IN THE ZONE II

IN THE ZONE II

Secrets of a World Champ

LEE SCHRANER

DEDICATION

To David J. Bryant CBE, my idol and hero, the greatest man who ever graced a bowling green. We only met once, but your friendliness, skill, sportsmanship, and love for lawn bowls made me want to become a champion just like you

Rest in Peace 27/10/1931 – 27/8/2020

Front Cover:
Lee Schraner kissing the World Champion of Champions perpetual trophy at Adelaide Bowling Club in 2019, shortly after defeating Hong Kong's Tony Cheung in a thrilling tie-break in the gold medal match

Photo Credit:
Paul Wilson and Adelaide Bowling Club

CONTENTS

Dedication v
Introduction xi

A
CRITICAL THEORIES OF MENTAL TOUGHNESS   **1**

  1 Gaining a Desired Result   2
  2 Victim Theory   7
  3 The Law of Attraction   15
  4 Conditioning   24
  5 Courage   30
  6 Choice   35

B
ESTABLISHED THEORIES OF MENTAL TOUGHNESS   **41**

  7 Experience   42
  8 Confidence   46

9	Motivation	51
10	Momentum	54
11	Conversation	59
12	Human Nature	69

C
ATTITUDE 75

13	Internal Dialogue	76
14	Self-Belief	83
15	Positive Thinking	90
16	Eliminating Negative Thoughts	95
17	Body Language	101
18	Concentration	109

D
PLANNING 115

19	SMART Goals	116
20	Developing a Game Plan	123
21	Comfort Zone	129

E
PERSONALITY 135

22	Preparation	136

	23	Routine	141
	24	Training	147
	25	Visualisation of Shot-Play	154
	26	Superstition	157

F
STRESS — **161**

	27	Anxiety	162
	28	Adrenaline	169
	29	Anger Management	173

G
SUCCESS & FAILURE — **179**

	30	Lessons of Failure	180
	31	Managing Success	187
	32	Winning, Losing & Review	193
	33	Selection	200
	34	Form	206

H
SKILLS & CHARACTER — **211**

	35	Leadership	212
	36	Personal Limits	221

37	Match Tempo	224
38	Exercise & Fitness	229
39	Sportsmanship & Respect	233

Conclusion 237
About the Author 241

INTRODUCTION

So, you want to become a better lawn bowler? You have come to the right place.

We are not here to discuss footwork, grass-line, bowls delivery or how to read a head. There are numerous coaching books available to help you make those decisions and plenty of qualified club coaches to help you with practical issues. We are here to 'think outside the square' and discover why mental toughness will positively impact your level of success.

In the Zone II – Secrets of a World Champ is designed to assist everybody from the ordinary club social bowler to the sport's most elite. It specifically targets areas outside the normal realms of coaching, making it the most unique lawn bowling publication on the market.

In the Zone – Developing Mental Toughness in Lawn Bowls was the number one selling lawn bowls book in the world on Amazon Kindle from 2014 to 2020. For those who have read the first edition, you are aware that we delved into unchartered waters and introduced new theories and hypotheses. I proposed topics and theories that were common by name but had little or no appreciation in the bowling world.

For those who are unaware, I was diagnosed with Severe General Anxiety Disorder (GAD) and Clinical Depression (CD) in 2003 at the age of 21. Being painful for many years, I was forced to make my mental health and well-being my number one priority in life. Since that diagnosis, I have researched psychological theories and practices to teach myself how to live with mental illness. I am not a qualified psychologist or even a counsellor, but what I discovered and later instilled, clearly saved my life.

On top of my research, I have been professionally treated in the areas of Cognitive Behavioural Therapy (CBT), Acceptance and Commitment Therapy (ACT) and Mindfulness. By combining research, therapy, and my sport of choice, I have been able to compile an in-depth text on mental toughness in lawn bowls.

Over time, this study and research was slowly introduced to my game. The positive change in my performance and results were evident almost immediately. I took the view that any approach that made my everyday life better, had to make my game of bowls better.

Make no mistake, my mental toughness is far from perfect. I still 'stuff-up' and commit silly errors from time to time. Human nature decides how I feel and think, and sometimes I forget I have a choice in the way I react. Part of the learning process is to identify these mistakes and understand how to rectify them moving forward.

Topics such as 'The Law of Attraction', 'Victim Theory' and 'Courage', have had significant input in the way I play, my attitude, and the way I feel.

I have learnt to set clear goals and how to best determine the processes and routine needed to achieve those goals.

I am conditioned to make willpower and mindful choices and to take advantage of my experience to make the right decisions.

My internal dialogue is sound. My positive thinking has helped me to eliminate negative thoughts and to absorb the self-belief needed to succeed.

I have studied anxiety, anger management, and dealing with failure, all to give me clear guidelines on commanding my feelings, emotions, and reactions.

I have also taught myself about individual skills such as leadership and match tempo, and how the use of these characteristics can determine my level of a performance.

I am a creator, not a victim. My understanding of the drama triangle and the empowerment dynamic have helped me avoid self-pity, poor excuses, and lacklustre justification for poor attitude.

I am a realist that feels at one with nature and the world. I honestly believe that 'like attracts like', that I cannot be a 'separate-self', and that if my life is not perfect, I can certainly attempt to perfect what is in it.

I am in a better place now, not just in bowls but in life.

This publication will not be without its sceptics. There may be theories discussed that you may disagree with, or you find completely irrelevant to your game of bowls. The only thing I ask is that you take the text for what it is, read it with an open mind, and understand that I put pen to paper because I know it works. If just one topic in this book improves your game, then I know this creation has been worthwhile.

I have always said that my ability never reached the heights of elite bowlers, but my mental toughness allowed me to compete against (and often beat) the best bowlers in the world.

Seventeen years of mental reconfiguration led me to a World Champion of Champions Gold Medal in Adelaide in 2019. I had the privilege of singing the Australian National Anthem in front of my mother, best friend, and an incredible group of supportive spectators. Everything I researched, studied, learnt, and applied, had sent me on a journey to the top of the world. The proof is in the pudding.

PART A

Critical Theories of Mental Toughness

CHAPTER 1

Gaining a Desired Result

Gaining a desired result is the process of setting a goal, understanding the process required to achieve that goal, and following a set routine.

One of the critical theories of mental toughness is the concept of gaining a desired result. To understand this concept, you need to break-down the elements of the theory. Namely:
- Setting a goal;
- Understanding the process; and
- Following a routine

Setting a Goal

Goal setting is discussed in detail later in this book, but for the purpose of this section, you need to be aware the following:
- Goals can be short-term, mid-term or long-term;
- Goals need to be Specific, Measurable, Achievable, Realistic and Timely (SMART); and
- Any set goal triggers a process, leading you to an increased probability of gaining a desired result

Understanding the Process

There is no point setting a goal unless you list the process required to achieve that goal.

You set goals to give yourself a direction or avenue to achievement. Once a goal is set, you need to outline the process required to achieve that goal.

As per the earlier example, there will be many processes required to achieve this goal.

Processes that may need to change or improve could involve:
- Training requirements
- Working on your game plan
- Mental strength and self-confidence
- Health and fitness

Other processes will be automatic, where no conscious thought of the process is required. These are generally ordinary everyday life processes that all contribute to achieving your goal, such as putting on your club uniform, being on time for a match, or polishing your bowls.

As your experience develops, you will learn what processes work best for you.

Following a Routine

No matter what goal has been set, and what processes have been identified, the notion of gaining a desired result relies heavily on a set delivery routine. Without a deliberate, free-flowing routine, your chances of achieving your goal is limited.

This book has a whole section on 'Personality', with a dedicated chapter on 'routine'. Routine should not be confused with superstition or preparation, although it is possible for these to overlap. Your 'comfort zone' is made up of goals, processes, and a routine, that allow you to perform to the best of your ability.

Gaining a desired result will be referred to many times throughout this book. Often, it will revolve around short-term goals, and what you aim to achieve with every single shot you play.

Each shot you play has a goal. Why are you playing that shot? Are you trying to draw the shot, kill the end, or play a cover bowl?

Once 'why' is established, you can identify 'how' you will achieve the goal through process and routine. For most short-term goals, you rely heavily on your delivery routine. You follow a consistent, well-trained, and comfortable delivery, that allows you the best possible chance of executing the shot successfully.

Whether consciously or subconsciously, you:
- Set a goal (i.e. to draw a close bowl)
- Incorporate processes such as visualisation and self-belief
- Execute your delivery routine

By analysing what you are trying to achieve, you set the basis for your expected outcome or desired result. Although your result will not always be as you planned, you automatically create a mental recording of every situation and outcome. Over time your experience will develop, and your goals, processes, and routine can be adjusted as required. Through such trial and error, your experience expands and your decision making improves.

The whole theory of gaining a desired result is based on a heuristic approach. In other words, you use intelligent guesswork and trial by error learning, to establish experience in identifying what your desired result will be. Once you have the 'why' and 'how', you can apply your proven processes and delivery routine.

Over time you will learn to identify the best desired result or outcome available. Sometimes this may not be getting shot. Defending a vulnerable position on the head or taking your medicine in a bad lie, may ultimately become your goal.

At times, getting shot is the worst thing you can do, as it may open opportunities for your opposition. Further, a failure to identify and pre-empt your opposition's next shot, could also result in poor shot selection and a poor result.

Use the terminology of 'gaining a desired result' moving forward, as it will remind you to take mental notes of the set goal, processes, and outcome. This growth in intelligence or 'game smarts', will help you make better decisions moving forward. When visiting a head or considering what shot to play, you should ask yourself, "what is my desired result?"

Once you determine your desired outcome and work out the best way to achieve that outcome, you can enter the mat with full confidence in your decision and execute the shot to the best of your ability. This attitude will not guarantee success, but it will improve the percentage of achieving desired results. In the long-term, whether consciously or subconsciously, your game will definitely benefit.

CHAPTER 2

Victim Theory

One of the most critical theories of mental toughness, is the notion I refer to as "Victim Theory".

When referring to Victim Theory, I am not referring to the National Socialists, Austria, or anything to do with World War II. I am in fact, referring to the Karpman Drama Triangle that depicts the roles of a Victim, a Persecutor, and a Rescuer.

I often get varied feedback about this topic. Although difficult to grasp the roles and fundamentals of the theory at first, I honestly believe the understanding of this theory will change the way you not only look at lawn bowls, but the way you look at your life in general.

For me personally, this theory is the main reason for my development and change in attitude over the past two decades.

Even today, I look back on regrettable instances and use that as ammunition to be better in the present and the future. Developing my attitude is a work in progress and it should be the same for you too.

The Drama Triangle

Karpman's Theory assumes that there is 'conflict' between two or more people. I have made my own personal adjustments to the theory, including changing 'conflict' to 'drama event'.

A 'drama event' is any situation that triggers the drama triangle, whether there is conflict or not, and sometimes, there does not need to be a second person involved. In other words, the persecutor can be a situation and not necessarily another person.

Victim
A victim is someone who has the attitude of "Poor me!". They identify something that has happened (or is happening) that makes them feel helpless, victimised, oppressed, powerless and hopeless.

Persecutor
A victim places the blame on a persecutor, who can be a person, a situation or both.

Rescuer

Feeling emotionally unstable, the victim will seek a rescuer to share their problem, but will insist that despite this, their situation cannot be fixed. A rescuer will use your situation for their own gratification.

In summary, the drama triangle assumes that a victim will blame a persecutor for their problem and seek out a rescuer to justify their attitude and feelings.

So why is understanding Victim Theory important when it comes to mental toughness in bowls?

Every person who has ever played lawn bowls in the history of the world has been a victim at least once. If you disagree with this notion, then you are being naïve. Virtually all lawn bowlers have been a persecutor, and a large number have been a rescuer. Somewhere along the line, you have played a role in the drama triangle.

For example, you are playing a game of singles and your opposition gets a vile wick and turns the head from four down into three up, completely by fluke. Immediately, you become a victim.

In this instance, the situation of 'bad luck' and/or your opponent become persecutors.

You instantly seek a rescuer. You want someone to acknowledge, approve and justify your victimisation. This could be a marker, a spectator or anyone else in your immediate vicinity.

Emotionally charged as a victim, you throw your hands in the air at your rescuer and use verbal expletives, seeking some sort of acknowledgement. You want to unload the burden of your pain.

After the match, the rescuer goes inside the clubhouse and describes the situation to others, labelling you a bad sport for their own gratification. In the end, you as the victim are made to look even worse than your initial behaviour. The rescuer has now become a persecutor, which results in you seeking yet another rescuer, and the drama triangle continues to flow.

The Empowerment Dynamic

The only way to correct your attitude is to employ the 'empowerment dynamic'.

The dynamic changes the roles of all three participants in the drama triangle. If you can mentally change the roles of the three people involved, then you have a greater chance of avoiding victimisation.

In the empowerment dynamic, the victim becomes the creator, the persecutor becomes the challenger and the rescuer becomes the coach.

Creator

The creator is someone who takes the time to stop and think about what they want i.e. what is their desired result? The creator is goal-oriented and result-focused. They understand that problems will arise from time to time, but instead of blaming a persecutor for their drama, they see the situation or person as a challenger.

Challenger

The challenger is a person or situation that forces you to reinforce your goals. The challenger must encourage you to focus on your goals and not on the problem at hand.

The role allows you to understand that a problem has occurred, and rather than playing the blame game or getting emotional, a creator will identify the problem as a challenge or 'small bump in the road', on the way to achieving your goals.

Coach

A coach is a lot different from a rescuer. They believe that the creator is an individual who can make the right attitude choices, is outcome driven, and can focus on the end goal.

The coach asks a number of questions that enables an individual to focus on what they want, instead of paying attention to current emotions. The coach is an equal to a creator. They help understand that the situation or challenger, is merely an obstacle attempting to derail you from your end goal.

It is possible for a creator to also be their own coach.

To become your own coach, you must have the skill to identify when you are falling (or about to fall) victim to a persecutor. If you refer to the earlier example, the wick has occurred and you have gone from four shots up, to three shots down. You immediately feel dejected and upset over the situation. You are in the process of falling victim and must trigger the empowerment dynamic.

Ask yourself these 3 simple questions:
 1) Can I change what just happened?
 2) It is in my best interests to think about what just happened?
 3) Is my health and temperament bettered by what just happened?

You will generally answer "no" to these three questions. By stopping and asking yourself these three simple questions, you have automatically triggered the role of a coach. This should allow you to become a creator, and not a victim. The creator will understand that this is just a short-term problem and will not let it de-rail you from your eventual goal or desired result. You will be able to brush the challenger aside and direct your focus back on the task at hand. You have avoided becoming a victim.

By applying the empowerment dynamic, the original example is over-turned. You are playing a game of singles and your opposition gets a vile wick, and turns the head from four down into three up. You become the coach and ask yourself the three temperament questions, answering "no" to all three.

You identify yourself as the creator and that this event is caused by a challenger who is trying to deter you from your overall goals. You identify the challenger as a short-term problem and can brush the challenger aside like water off a duck's back. You have avoided becoming a victim.

Over time you will develop your skills in this area and have the mental capacity to avoid falling victim to a persecutor. When feeling as though you are about to fall victim, you will initiate the coach and turn yourself into a creator. Any hindrance to your overall goals will always be a challenge. You should never again feel like the world is against you.

A Constant Reminder of the Victim

Over many years, I have encouraged the practical use of this theory in a team environment. We can all slip up from time to time and it may be up to our peers to coach us into the empowerment dynamic.

I instruct players to vocally label a team-mate a 'victim' if they believe it is necessary to do so. The labelled player may first be offended but will quickly realise that their team-mate has taken on the role of a coach, refusing to rescue them.

Victims are not welcome in a team environment, as they bring the whole team down.

This verbal label should automatically trigger the empowerment dynamic and the victim must take on the role of the creator. A great team-mate should respect and understand why they have been labelled a victim, and have the decency to keep the team goals ahead of their own emotions and agenda. Remember, as a creator you must realise that whatever happened is just a little bump on the road to your end goals.

The empowerment dynamic at its absolute best.

The main secret to a successful team environment is unlocked. Coach it! Use it!

CHAPTER 3

The Law of Attraction

The 'Law of Attraction' is a completely new section from the first edition, but in my opinion, so important that it has become a critical theory.

Without trying to prove complicated psychodynamics or detailed Laws of the Universe, I want you to understand the basics of this law and how it can improve your game. At times in this chapter, we will delve into areas that you may never have even thought of or discussed.

All I ask is that you read it with an open mind.

This Law is not simple. You simply cannot just imagine 'something' and then suddenly that 'something' appears. Unfortunately, many people who have attempted to apply this law to their daily lives have failed through lack of patience and understanding. Considering the purpose of this Law can improve your life, if applied correctly, it can certainly improve your mental toughness in sport.

I attribute my World Singles Title to the Law of Attraction. Trust me, it works!

The three laws of attraction are:
1) Like attracts Like
2) Nature abhors a vacuum
3) The present is always perfect

Like Attracts Like

What you think about and believe, you generally do. Your thoughts can suggest actions, which produce an outcome. This is human nature.

Forget about the term 'opposites attract'. This may be relevant to a magnet, but most of the time 'similarities attract'. If you want to attract 'something' or achieve, you need to modify your thoughts and mindset to draw that 'something' closer.

In bowls, you want to compete at the best level possible, giving yourself the greatest chance of achieving your goals or desired results.

So where do you start?

If 'like attracts like' then positive thoughts attract positive outcomes, while negative thoughts attract negative outcomes. There are detailed sections on positive thoughts and eliminating negative thoughts later in this book.

If 'like attracts like' then a good attitude attracts good people, while a bad attitude attracts bad people.

If 'like attracts like' then victims attract rescuers, while challengers attract coaches.

If you want to become more attractive, you must learn to remove anything that might make you a repellent.

A lack of motivation will attract others with a lack of motivation – so motivate yourself!

A poor training effort will attract others with a poor training effort – so train harder and smarter than ever before!

A lack of success will attract others with a lack of success – so get out there and win something!

The idea of 'like attracts like' is purely an attitude choice. You can condition yourself to have a winning attitude. A winning attitude leads to winning. Even in losing, your attitude should remain focused on learning from your loss, and how to win next time. I discuss 'conditioning' in detail later in this section.

If what you think about and what you believe in is generally what you attract, then why not think about the good things in life?

It can't hurt right?

Nature Abhors a Vacuum

Don't let the name of the second law fool you. This law is simple to understand, but will take you a lifetime to master.

'Abhor' means a hatred or disgust. If nature 'abhors' something, it rejects it.

The definition of a vacuum is a true empty space devoid of matter – an environment with nothing in it. So, if 'nature abhors a vacuum', then 'nature rejects a true empty space' and fills it.

A true vacuum cannot exist in nature, because as soon as 'nothing' is created, nature fills it with something else, or it collapses.

Complicated? Stay with me here, it is all about to make sense.

Your 'self' is everything in nature and everything it experiences in its world. You are the environment, the land, the people. You are the whole world. If you try to separate yourself from everything, you attempt to create a vacuum that instantly collapses.

Any attempt to separate yourself from nature and to create a 'separate self' is so fragile and unstable that it disappears. A 'separate self' cannot naturally exist. If you feel cut off from the world, you are mistaken.

A 'self' longs for many things in life. You may want money, relationships, power, authority, and good health, just to name a few. You try so hard to fill these so-called voids, that if you experience failure, you are more likely to abuse alcohol, drugs, yourself, and other people. This law says that attempting to fill voids in your life is a pointless exercise, because you are everything already.

Now, here is where the magic kicks in.

You are one with nature, as am I. You cannot be a separate self, nor can I. Chasing needs and wants is a waste of time. You already have everything. You are everything. Your 'self' is nature. You might think you are filling a void, but you aren't. Are you on an endless life quest to fill something that is already full? Are driving yourself into a madness of endless wants and needs? Why try and fill a void that doesn't exist?

Do you want the meaning of happiness? Well here it is.

No matter how bad you think life is, it will always be special. It is your life. For this reason, you should always be at peace with your 'self'. Don't knock yourself for failing to fill non-existent voids. Understanding that voids cannot exist should free you from self-hate. You cannot fill something that is not there, so don't be your own worst enemy.

You should walk onto a bowling green as one with nature. You are the green, the bowls, the mat, the jack, the spectators. You are the world.

From this place of peace, anything is possible. No needs or wants. No beginning or end. Nothing to look for. No void to fill. Nature has nothing to abhor. There are no voids and no vacuum.

You now live in a bliss of happiness. There is no separate self. There never was and there never will be.

Can you feel the power of your 'self' with nature? The aura of nature is magnificent. Your 'self' is wonderful. Not a worry in the world. You can relax in your natural world instead of trying to fight against it.

What an epiphany!

The Present is Always Perfect

The third law of attraction teaches that the 'present is perfect', even if you think it isn't.

There are bad things happening every day around the world which may make you think that the present isn't perfect at all; in fact, far from it.

To activate this law, you must make your current reality as perfect as possible.

If there are things in your life that you hate right now, remember that you have a choice. Eliminate the negative and replace with a positive or learn to perfect what you already have. Worrying about the past or future is futile. Living takes place in the present.

Under the third law of attraction, you take the view that if something about yourself isn't perfect right now, then you can make it perfect.

If you want the perfect training regime, perfect the one you already have.

If you want the perfect attitude, perfect the one you already have.

If you want the perfect bowls delivery, perfect the one you already have – go and see a coach.

Remember the first law of attraction; like attracts like.

You need to take this law in its simplest terms. Either:
   - You are already perfect; or

- If something about you is not perfect, you can perfect it (or at least try to)

The Law of Attraction in reality

I attribute the success of my World Champion of Champions Gold Medal to the Law of Attraction. It helped me understand that if I wanted to become a World Champion, I had to live it, breathe it, and definitely believe it.

I had to attract positive things into my life by eliminating negative thoughts and replacing them with positive thoughts.

I had to understand that there was no such thing as a 'separate-self', and that I was the green, the bowls, the mat, my surroundings, the jack, and that I already had everything I needed to be a champion.

I believed that my present was perfect, and anything that did not appear to be perfect, was perfected, until it was perfect.

I had successfully applied the three Laws of Attraction to my life and honestly believed that the theory could not fail.

It might have taken seventeen years for my thoughts to become a reality in the eyes of others, but in my own mind I was already there. I had visualised the dais, the gold medal, heard the National Anthem so many times before, and believed it so much to be reality, that it just had to happen.

The actual living moment had an eerie sense of 'deja vu'. I had seen this all before.

The Law of Attraction at its best.

CHAPTER 4

Conditioning

Your attitude is a set of beliefs, emotions and behaviour towards people, objects, and situations. How you react defines your attitude.

Conditioning is a process you undertake to correct or change your attitude. In sport, attitude is everything. The whole concept of mental toughness requires an attitude of belief and understanding. To improve your attitude, you must believe and understand conditioning.

The popular saying 'think before you act' means to 'assess your attitude before reacting'. Human nature decides how you feel about a situation, so you need to pause for a few brief seconds and assess your attitude before reacting. This is a lot trickier than it sounds.

All bowlers can recall times when a poor attitude resulted in poor behaviour. God knows that I have had my fair share over time!

Sometimes your emotions boil over and your body releases the tension. Unfortunately, once you have calmed down and returned to nature, you instantly regret your behaviour.

The key to conditioning your attitude is to limit the number of times your behaviour reacts adversely to a situation. There are ways to expand a positive attitude and supress and dilute a negative attitude. Attitude can be conditioned to change.

The three main types of attitude conditioning are:
    1) Classical conditioning
    2) Operant or Instrumental Conditioning
    3) Observational Conditioning

Classical Conditioning

Classical conditioning from the outside, may appear as child's play, but it is extremely effective. It involves pairing a potent stimulus with a neutral stimulus, to create a positive reflex or positive reaction.

Although complex in detail, this theory can be simplified and related to not only lawn bowls, but your everyday life.

As an example, a song could be classified as a neutral stimulus. To most everyday human beings, a song is just a song.

An example of a potent stimulus is concentration, as it increases mental exertion and thought.

If you pair a certain song with concentration, you can use the music to stimulate concentration at any given point in time.

A lot of sports stars around the world can be seen listening to headphones immediately prior to a match. It is likely that such music, sounds, or content, is classically conditioning them for the game ahead. The music is stimulating something potent like concentration, focus, or energy. It might also be to ignore nerves and to inspire courage.

There are many neutral stimuli that you can use to trigger potent stimuli. I use the notion of the 'three bells', where my brain automatically signals a red alert when I make the same mistake with three bowls in a row. This clear sound of "Ding! Ding! Ding!" stimulates my concentration. It is a clear time for me to slow down, assess the three previous mistakes, and execute a correction. The 'three bells' theory is something I have used in my game for over 20 years and will continue to always use.

Operant or Instrumental Conditioning

Operant conditioning involves reward or punishment for behaviour. You use this type of conditioning to train your pets and to teach your children, but it is also extremely effective for adults.

You can use operant conditioning to modify your own attitude. As simple as it sounds, rewarding yourself for a good attitude and good behaviour will extrinsically motivate you to keep doing so. Alternatively, punishment for a bad attitude or bad behaviour will discourage you from repeating this in the future.

As an example, I will reward myself with a beautiful dinner and nice glass of gin when my attitude has positively influenced my performance in a match.

On the other hand, I will force myself to read three chapters of this book, when I have let a situation adversely affect my attitude. I will also skip the nice glass of gin with dinner. Although I use this book as a reference point regularly, sitting down and re-reading three chapters is a punishment and reminder that a bad attitude is not acceptable under any circumstances.

You might think that such conditioning is immature and childish, but it works. I cannot tell you how much I miss that nice gin when my attitude and behaviour has taken a nose-dive. I even sit the bottle on the dinner table while eating as a reminder.

If you want operant conditioning to work for you, then reward yourself for each day of positive attitude, and don't forget to punish yourself when your attitude negatively influences your game. You will honestly be surprised by the results.

Observational Conditioning

Observational conditioning is exactly as it sounds. It is the observation of the behaviour of others that can directly influence your own behaviour and attitude.

To apply observational conditioning, you need to focus on your bowling mentors and heroes and take note of their attitude. The best bowlers in the world may have incredible skill and ability, but no-one makes it to the top with a bad attitude.

Take David Bryant as an example. He won four consecutive Commonwealth Games Gold Medals in singles. His attitude, behaviour, skill, and sportsmanship were all on display. He is the perfect hero for any up and coming lawn bowler.

If you surround yourself with bad attitudes, you are likely to develop one yourself. You will see yourself as a victim and constantly rely on rescuers to justify your attitude. Your attitude may also get even worse than what it already is.

Sometimes I exit a conversation with others and move to an area by myself. It isn't to avoid social contact with a table of people or bowlers, it is to remove myself from a toxic discussion. I refuse to sit and be part of chats that may adversely impact my own attitude. I am conditioned to observe positive attitudes and such negativity is removed from my life as much as possible.

If you can apply at least one form of conditioning to your game, then you are taking the first steps towards improving your attitude and behaviour. I suggest starting with just one method, adopting a second and third only when the previous one becomes habit.

Your attitude could be the difference between winning and losing, so take the time to condition yourself. If your attitude is not perfect, we must attempt to perfect the one you already have.

CHAPTER 5

Courage

Of all the chapters in this book, courage is certainly my favourite. There are so many great quotes about courage, and each one can be an inspiration for snatching victory from the jaws of defeat.

Mark Twain once said that "Courage is resistance to fear, mastery of fear".

Margaret Mitchell was known to say on many occasions that "With enough courage, you can do without a reputation".

My most favourite quote about courage comes from World icon Nelson Mandela, who said "I learned that courage was not the absence of fear, but the triumph over it. The brave man is not he who does not feel afraid, but he who conquers that fear".

When talking about courage, you must understand the feeling of fear. Everyone is likely to get scared or nervous at one time or another. On the bowling green, there are many times you will feel your nerves begin to kick in. So how do you find the courage to overcome whatever it is that has made you scared?

Courage is a **willingness** to confront fear, uncertainty, and intimidation. It is the ability to take a given situation front on and to do something about it. It is the skill to find power, resistance, and strength when all feels lost and hopeless.

I learnt courage through poor health, but now I adopt it in every single game of bowls I play. Australian representative Aaron Teys once said to me that he "hated" playing against me (even though he had just beaten me), because he knows from first bowl to last that he is "in for it". He knows that despite the score-line of any game, I will use my courage to never give up.

In lawn bowls, we mostly use what is known as 'moral courage'.

As a sign of positive body language, moral courage is the will to stand up when everybody else wants you to sit down.

It is the will to go on when everyone else has given up.

It is to continually battle, even in a fight about to be lost.

Courage cannot be under-estimated in sport, especially lawn bowls. A courageous opponent will make you earn every single shot, keeping you on your toes for hours on end.

A courageous opponent will always maintain at least a perseverant level of confidence and will never accept defeat.

A courageous opponent will never fall victim to a persecutor or a negative situation. They have their focus on their end goals and are not distracted by obstacles that may come across their path.

A courageous opponent will show grace and skill under pressure. They are quite simply the example of what every bowler strives to be.

I am sure most bowlers have had a come from behind win when all seemed lost. Most have also led by large amounts and crumbled to a devastating defeat. It is an amazing feeling when you gather back all your lost shots and sneak home in a thriller. It is also horrific when the game is in the bag and out of nowhere, you lose the unlosable!

I want you to think about a time when you were dead and buried in a game and found the courage to never give up; a time when you realised that a miracle was needed and you actually achieved one. Isn't it the best feeling? That is not luck, that is courage.

Courage gives you the opportunity to walk off the bowling green knowing that you gave everything you had, despite the final result. It allows you to walk away standing tall and free from regrets. It basically gives you the right to feel good after every game no matter how many you won or lost by.

Courage is this inner super-power that allows you to achieve all the time, every time. It makes you feel good about yourself and increases your overall enjoyment for the sport.

If you are willing to give your best 100% of the time during every game you play, then you are as courageous as you can possibly be. You give yourself every possible chance of winning and can guarantee that you will never give up.

If you walk away from a game knowing you could have done better, then you are not courageous. You will feel awful about yourself and the match and most likely be ill-tempered and frustrated. You will have regrets.

Courage is about excluding all regrets from your game. It provides a clear avenue to enjoyment and success.

A courageous bowler is not lucky when they win the close games, they deserve them.

A courageous bowler who comes from behind and records an amazing victory, or holds off a fast finishing opponent while staying cool under pressure, deserves every win they have.

The most memorable wins are the tough games that require every iota of courage to get over the line. It is not the easy wins or the biggest wins that you remember, it is the wins that when everybody else chewed their nails, or sat down and gave up, you stood up and faced your fears.

Make the choice to be courageous. One day you might need to draw a shot within a foot of a sunken jack to win a World Singles.

Nervous? A little.

Courage? Without a doubt.

CHAPTER 6

Choice

Do you know how many choices you make every single day, whether consciously or subconsciously? My research indicates that an average adult makes approximately 35,000 choices on a daily basis.

You make so many choices that often you don't even realise you make them. Something as simple as choosing which sock to put on first when getting dressed, can easily be done completely devoid of thought, yet a choice is made.

For the purpose of this section, I want to focus on conscious choices and in particular, choices that will improve your performance on the bowling green.

A conscious choice is a choice you make that is morally, practically, and ethically right according to your own conscience.

Believe it or not, you make hundreds of conscious choices in every game of bowls you play. For example, the most obvious conscious choice you make in a game of singles, is what shot to play.

You make choices about length of play, what hand to play, when to cover, when to attack, when to walk up and look at the head etc. These examples are all obvious practical conscious choices.

A lawn bowler will gain a clear advantage over any opponent when they can not only make good practical conscious choices, but when they can start to make choices that involve willpower and mindfulness.

Willpower Choices

Willpower is the ability to overcome unwanted thoughts, emotions, and temptations, to focus on the achievement of goals and desired results. A willpower choice is one you make so that you can avoid reacting to unwanted thoughts, emotions, and temptations. You set goals to ensure that the choices you make are purely focused on achieving your goal.

Willpower choices define your attitude. For example, you might make the willpower choice today to improve your knowledge of Victim Theory, because you know that understanding the empowerment dynamic will help you become a better creator. As you have already learnt, a creator understands that a challenger is only a small bump in the road on the way to your end goals. Being a creator is a willpower choice.

You can make a lot of willpower choices that have a positive influence on your game. These choices can be made as soon as you are ready. Many topics in this book rely on you making a willpower choice. Even the introduction of just one theory may make you not only a better bowler, but a better human being.

If you want a better attitude, learn how to condition yourself. Make the willpower choice to have a better attitude.

If you want to be free of nerves and increase your courage, learn to face your fears. Make the willpower choice to become courageous.

If you want to work on your temperament, then study anger management. Make the choice to control your temper.

Picture yourself at a crossroads with your career. Don't simply go through the motions. Willpower is about you. You decide your path.

Mindful Choices

Mindful choices are decisions in the present that are made thoughtfully, rather than by impulse or outside influences.

This type of choice is especially important during a match.

It is easy to be frustrated and annoyed and to make rash choices based on emotion, impulse or negative influences. A true champion is able to stop, analyse the situation and make a thoughtful choice.

During a match there will be many ups and downs or ebbs and flows. Winning a close match may be decided by the player who makes mindful choices.

Don't get yourself into a situation where you walk off after a match and say, "I should have done this, or I should have done that". That is a natural human reaction to a game you have just lost. Knowing that you made mindful choices throughout the entire game and executed your game plan to the best of your ability, allows you to absorb the result free from regret.

It is okay post-match to be emotionally thrilled or disappointed. Once the result is final, there is nothing you can do to change it. Be mindful that your pleasure can be your opponent's pain and vice versa. Make the choice to be graceful in victory and defeat.

If you can make conscious practical choices, positive willpower choices and mindful choices, you increase the chances of achieving your goals and desired results.

Ultimately, you must admit that you can do better. Once you discover this realisation you can 'draw a line in the sand' and begin making better choices. The past may be the best indicator of the future, but it is not a guarantee. You can influence your present to set a pathway to a better future. Being a better bowler is a choice.

PART B

Established Theories of Mental Toughness

CHAPTER 7

Experience

Experience is a term often used loosely to provide an excuse for someone who has just been beaten on the green. Is appears to be a justifiable excuse for a bowler who made mistakes in a match that ultimately contributed to them losing.

What many bowlers fail to understand is the clear distinction between 'experience' and 'excuses'. The definition of an idiot is someone who continually does the same thing over and over again, expecting a different outcome. An idiot is someone who uses excuses.

Have you ever heard the phrase "You can't buy experience?"

There are many different theories surrounding experience. Some of the great philosophers have provided their own distinct definition:

Aristotle once said, "For the things we have to learn before we can do them, we learn by doing them".

Oprah Winfrey has been heard to say, "Turn your wounds into wisdom".

Randy Pausch stated in 'The Last Lecture', "Experience is what you get when you didn't get what you wanted and it is often the most valuable thing you have to offer".

Even the great Henry Ford said, "The only real mistake is the one from which we learn nothing".

But my favourite of all quotes regarding experience comes from Oscar Wilde who once said, "Nothing that is worth knowing can be taught".

When considering experience, there is one main trend that always makes an appearance and that is 'learning'. Let the game teach you something each time you play and learn to adapt to situations that arise.

My theory on experience is simple: Experience is something you gain or learn from a situation where you knew you could have done better. In other words, given your time over again, what would you have done better?

In lawn bowls, you often see many new bowlers entering club championships in their early years and being well beaten by the more experienced players. What the newer bowlers learn is invaluable moving forward. If they do not participate in events beyond their current level of skill, then they will learn nothing.

Even the most experienced bowlers will learn new things every time they train or play a match. They could survive a close shave with a less prominent opponent or even lose a match they should have won. Rather than falling victim to the situation, the bowler must review their performance and expand their experience.

There can be many reasons why an upset can occur. Your opposition may have played better under the conditions, you could have had an 'off' day, or a mixture of both.

Understanding and pin-pointing the exact reasons, will ensure that given the same situation again, you will have experience to rely upon to help you get through. Learning from a match will develop your overall experience levels.

When asking yourself "What could I have done better?" you are able to pinpoint exact situations and develop your own experience.

There is generally more than one factor as to why your performance is below par. These can include:
- Becoming a victim
- Poor preparation
- Lethargy
- Dehydration
- Failure to concentrate

- Not executing a game plan
- Impatience
- Poor shot selection

As much as it hurts a bowler to sit down after a match and review a loss or substandard performance, it will better your match play in the long run.

When you apply techniques or tactics in a game, to rectify a bad situation, you are using your experience.

Remembering a previous situation that may arise again and knowing how to avoid a similar result is experience.

Knowing how to dig yourself out of trouble in a tough match is experience.

Pin-pointing the reasons why you are playing below par in a match is experience.

You may suffer some heart-breaking losses or make some poor decisions in your bowling career, but if you can learn from your mistakes, you are developing your experience.

Using your experience during match play will keep you 'in the zone' and increase your chances of gaining a desired result.

CHAPTER 8

Confidence

Confidence is probably one of the widest terms used in sport today. For the purpose of lawn bowls, we will specifically discuss 'self-confidence'.

Self-Confidence is having (or showing) confidence in oneself. It is the ability to have faith and belief in your game plan, decisions, and execution. It is the feeling that you can achieve your set goals.

In my opinion, Hawthorn and St Kilda legend Allan Jeans provides the best theory on confidence. He classifies confidence into three levels:
1. Supreme
2. Perseverance
3. Acceptance

Supreme

Supreme confidence is where you are the freight train. Anything that stands on the track in front of you is demolished. You are playing above your own ability level and every shot you attempt appears to be coming off. Generally, you are well in front on the scoreboard.

Perseverance

Perseverance is like a set of scales. The game is in the balance. You are neither playing brilliant or terrible and you are trying your best to reach the supreme level of confidence.

Acceptance

Acceptance is when you are the little lamb on the tracks about to be hit by the freight train. You have accepted defeat in all regard and have virtually stopped trying. You have fallen victim to the persecutor and are awaiting your last rights in a match.

The reason confidence is classified as an established theory of mental toughness, is because it is a well-known term that you need to understand. You need to know how to control your emotions and how to adapt and execute your game plan through each of the three stages.

When supreme, there is only one danger you need to be aware of. You must never over-exaggerate your ability by taking shortcuts, lairising, or becoming over-confident. This attitude could lead to a stray from your game plan and result in avoidable mistakes. Such errors could mean losing supremacy in a match and dropping to a perseverant or accepting level of confidence. Yes, it is great to have supreme confidence, but never let it detract you from the result you are trying to achieve or the goal you are pursuing.

When persevering, you are fighting as hard as you can to stay in a match. Your aim is to reach the supreme level of confidence and this is often achieved through the will to persevere and 'fight it out'. Scoreboard pressure aside, you must always persevere toward your desired result or end goal. Even if the match appears diabolical, a modification to your game plan is a way of demonstrating perseverance. Never accept the situation for what it is. You can always do something to try and change it; change the length, become more aggressive or alter the current tempo of a game.

Once you have reached the acceptance level of confidence, you will make excuses, blame others, and fall victim to the persecutor. You will seek somebody to rescue you from your own self-pity and sadness. You have given up on the game and will most likely get well-beaten. If you ever fall to this level of confidence, you should seriously re-consider your goals and desires in the sport. No-one should ever fall to this level of confidence, because even when all seems lost, a hint of courage might lift you back into perseverance.

Confidence can be internal and external.

In a team environment, you should always ensure that your external confidence is showing, even if your internal confidence is low.

As a singles player, your external confidence can influence the attitude of yourself and your opposition and should always be positive.

Simply 'acting confident' externally, you can trick yourself and our opposition into believing that you are supreme or at least perseverant in confidence. In other words, despite the scoreline, you continue to exude confidence, indicating that you will never give up.

I call this 'mirage confidence'.

Mirage confidence provides an aura and positive attraction to your team-mates, even when the chips are down. Others can feed off your attitude and their own confidence can grow. Even if playing singles, the external actions alone can improve your own internal confidence.

When at the perseverance level of confidence, simply acting confident or demonstrating mirage confidence could be the difference between winning and losing. It will keep your body language upbeat, will show leadership and will grab the attention of your team-mates, opposition, and spectators. It could make you the centre of attention and provide positive distraction to your nervous team-mates and an annoying distraction to your opposition. One great shot may be all it takes to send your whole team into supreme confidence.

Even if mirage confidence does not get the result, at least you can walk off the green with your head held high, knowing you did all you could. In the end, that attitude choice of 'having a go' will leave you at peace, with no regrets.

CHAPTER 9

Motivation

Motivation is the driving force to achieve your goals and desired results. It is the will and desire to succeed. It is a behaviour that encourages positive direction and well-being. It is the crux of why we play sport.

Motivation is divided into two types:
- Intrinsic motivation (internal); and
- Extrinsic motivation (external)

Intrinsic Motivation

Intrinsic motivation is motivation driven by enjoyment and interest in a specific task. It exists without the need for reward and outcome. It is the motivation of wanting to do something, even if it is only for self-pleasure.

The love for the sport of lawn bowls is an intrinsic motivation that should encourage the will to succeed extrinsically.

I believe intrinsic motivation is implied for all lawn bowlers as ultimately, we play sport for enjoyment. To develop mentally, the focus needs to be placed on extrinsic motivation.

Extrinsic Motivation

Extrinsic motivation is driven by external factors such as rewards, money, and trophies. It also includes applause, recognition, and the achievement of desired results.

To be motivated extrinsically, you need incentives. Luckily in bowls, there are always rewards for winners. Whether playing social bowls, playing in club championships, tournaments, State or National events, there are always incentives.

These incentives can also be classified as needs. Bowlers need the sense of achievement and success to be motivated to do better.

Motivational Needs

In lawn bowls, our needs are our goals. The setting and achievement of a goal or desired result will provide the motivation to set more challenging goals in the future. The success of latter goals will motivate you to challenge yourself even more.

For the purpose of lawn bowls, you need not know any other theories associated with motivation. You only need to recognise that intrinsically, you play the sport for the enjoyment, and that extrinsically you like to win, succeed, and achieve your goals.

If you ever lack in motivation, a change or review of your goals is the major source for sparking the motivation to succeed once again. Ironically, an increase in extrinsic motivation will directly increase your intrinsic motivation.

Why? Because you rather feel the joys of victory than the despair of defeat. Any objection to this notion goes against evolution and human nature.

CHAPTER 10

Momentum

The most over-used word in sport around the globe is the notion of 'momentum'.

Momentum is described as 'being on a roll' or when 'everything appears to be going right'. It is the supposed feeling that overwhelms you, gives rise to adrenalin and influences your level of confidence.

There are many theories associated with momentum and these theories often divide the greatest sporting coaches and minds. Some believe momentum to be one of the biggest influences on the performance of an individual or team, while others completely discount its impact.

The great argument asks one simple question:

Is momentum real, or is it just a cognitive illusion?

The concept of momentum is drilled into the sporting culture. It has been proven that athletes do feel and experience the perception of momentum. The key word here is 'perception'.

You will often perceive a point in a match where things are going well, and your confidence is supreme. On the reverse, it is often identifiable when things are not going so well, where you may become a victim and slip into the acceptance level of confidence. Quite often, you will refer to these situations as a 'change in momentum'.

Personally, I am in the minority when discussing perceived momentum. I am a true believer that momentum is self-implied and that it is a total and utter illusion. You may perceive momentum to shift away from you in any given match while at exactly the same time, one of your team-mates perceives that momentum has shifted in your favour.

Momentum is therefore, an opinion.

For example, your opposing skipper has drawn well all day and about half-way through the match, he plays a drive and puts the jack in the ditch. Your score is close, and this particular shot puts you behind on the scoreboard.

Your leader, second and third all slump their shoulders and perceive that the successful drive and change in score has shifted the momentum in the match.

You (the skip) on the other hand, are thrilled to see your opponent playing weight at the head. Even though he is successful, you perceive that the use of weight is against the skipper's natural play and might break the consistency of how well he was drawing. You believe that the momentum has swung in your favour.

How can it be possible that members of the same team perceive exact opposites?

If momentum is a perception and an opinion, then any perceived swing is generally driven by your own internal thoughts. In other words, individually.

You should never use momentum as an excuse to motivate a team or individual, as the term is widely misunderstood. Coaching a team to follow a game plan and to reach set goals, while also discussing the impacts of momentum, is totally contradictory. It just doesn't make sense and can confuse a bowler.

Momentum is quite simply the general ups and downs that occur in any given match.

Sometimes momentum is perceived to be with you longer and you are able to win. On the other hand, you may have the opinion that it is against you and you lose.

Momentum is an irrelevant thought that if against you, is likely to make you a victim and possibly send you into the acceptance level of confidence.

Momentum is totally over-rated and a self-perception that results in distraction from your end goals.

You are a creator and creators understand that any short-term problem (or perception of momentum shift) should not deter you from achieving your end goal or desired result. No matter what you perceive about momentum, it must be extinguished from your thoughts before it causes a distraction to your overall goals.

Genuinely believing in momentum will break your concentration and affect your focus on the task at hand.

By perceiving that momentum is with you, you are likely to make rash decisions, play over-confident shots, and stray from your game plan.

When feeling momentum is against you, you will also make rash decisions, play over-defensively, and stray from your game plan.

Either way, momentum is a total distraction from your game plan and goals and does nothing to strengthen your mental toughness. You must develop the ability to ignore momentum and keep a clear focus on achieving your desired result.

Any thought, perception or opinion that distracts you from your end goals is a detour to failure. Use your experience to follow your game plan and focus on the processes you need to follow to reach your goals.

Not everyone agrees with my theory on momentum, but at least you are now aware that momentum is only an individual perception and opinion. Anyone can have a different perception or opinion at any given point in time. Believing in momentum does nothing for team compatibility or goal congruence and if not ignored, can result in rash decision making and a poor performance.

I purely and honestly believe that momentum is the most misinformed and misunderstood concept in modern sport.

To be a better lawn bowler, you must learn to ignore any perceptions you have about momentum.

CHAPTER 11

Conversation

Conversation is verbal communication between two or more people. This type of communication is a common, everyday transaction, that can be formal or informal. It can be a quick exchange of words, or an in-depth discussion for hours on end.

Conversation is engaged when a transaction of words passes from one person to at least one other. What you say to engage conversation, or how you react to an engagement, can often decide the direction of a chat. The conversation can continue, end immediately, encourage conflict, or change direction.

As a coach, team leader, or skipper, you have an underlying responsibility to communicate effectively with each of your team-mates. What you say to your players individually and as a group, will have an impact on how they respond.

Group conversation is easier to control as generally you are the one doing the speaking. The obvious problem is that each individual will react differently to your message. Anyone who chooses to engage in a team conversation will do so to either support you, end it, disagree (and start a conflict), or attempt to change the direction of the conversation. When this occurs, you can then control the conversation by treating the engagement as a one-on-one talk.

Learning to control a conversation is a valuable skill, especially in a team environment. Whether in a group or one-on-one, you as the team leader must ensure your communication resonates with the majority.

You can control a one-on-one conversation by applying any of Eric Berne's 'three ego-states' of 'transactional analysis'.

Berne's Three Ego States

Eric Berne discovered that a person's ego could and would change over the course of a single conversation. He learnt that everyone played the same three roles at one time or another and that one person could control a conversation by applying the right ego at the right time.

Remembering that a conversation can continue, end immediately, encourage conflict, or change direction, Berne identified the three ego states as Parent, Child, and Adult. Further, he identified a conversational exchange as a 'transaction'. Finally, he stated that you consciously or unconsciously activate your ego states during a conversational transaction.

Parent

The 'parent' ego is a state where you rely on past roots of attitude, emotion, and behaviour, while engaging in conversation. The parent generally engages or responds based on what they were taught by their own parents. The parent acts with authority in a conversation and more often than not, delivers advice, control, and nurture.

A parent can be caring, loving or helpful, but also critical, authoritarian and a disciplinarian. Some people will react better to a nurturing parent, while others will respond better to a parent who exercises control. One of the great skills of coaching is to understand your conversation audience and know exactly what to say to each individual.

When using the ego state of a parent, you must take into consideration who the other person in the conversation is and how you want them to react. Unfortunately, the parent will often subconsciously choose their conversation based on past experiences and roots, without assessing the present situation.

Child

The 'child' ego is a state where you rely on past roots of thoughts, feelings, and behaviour, while engaging in conversation. The child will engage or respond based on impulse, spontaneity and needs, all part of a developed personality from younger years.

A child can be curious, interested, or innocent, but also guilty, scared, and immature. To avoid conflict, a child will often need the introduction of a parent or adult to the conversation.

If a child has a discussion with another child, it could be an innocent interaction of curiosity or interest. This type of conversation is generally between children under six years of age.

A Child vs Child interaction in the bowling world is almost guaranteed to form a conflict. If a conversation is started by a child through guilt, fear or immaturity, a responding child will transact on impulse with their own needs or beliefs. A conflict is created, where emotions are likely to form the basis for the conversation.

As an example, a child with no bowls remaining may express fear of a vulnerable back position on the rink. If a child responds, they will focus on their own needs or beliefs and say something like, "Well my bowls are counting, so someone else should have covered the back". Instantly there is conflict.

Adult

The 'adult' ego has the ability to thoughtfully analyse any present situation or conversation and to transact accordingly. An adult will identify the data present in both their inner-child and inner-parent, and in conjunction with gathered adult data, process, evaluate and validate the data to interact on a mature level.

Most of our daily conversations involve Adult vs Adult and a majority of these are done subconsciously. These conversations flow easily. For example, asking "How are you?", where you get a response of "I'm well thanks. How are you?", is a basic interpretation of two adults having a subconscious conversation.

An adult will often be required to respond to a child or parent, in order to gain control of a conversation. To better understand how this is done, you need to analyse the transaction.

Transactional Analysis

Transactional analysis is the evaluation of the egos used (or about to be used) in a conversation. A 'transaction' is made up of three parts of the conversation, namely:
1) The conversation stimulus (and the ego state used to activate it)
2) The response (and the ego state) you are expecting to receive
3) The response you receive (and the ego state that comes with it)

Complementary Transactions

If you stimulate a conversation, you may expect a response similar to the one you receive. This is known as a 'complementary' transaction.

A complementary transaction is one where a conversation is initiated by an ego, where the response received by the other ego, is what you were expecting to receive. Both egos need to be complementary or sympathetic to each other. This type of transaction is described as the most effective type of verbal communication.

For example:

You initiate a conversation using a parent ego. You tell a team mate to not drink alcohol before a game as it negatively impacts skill and judgement. You are expecting to receive a response from a scared child ego, who relies upon their past roots, knowing that alcohol is not good for their body.

Your expected response is ratified. The child responds by apologising for their pre-match drinking and says they will not do it again in the future.

Crossed Transactions

On the other hand, your initial communication may deliver a response completely different to what you were expecting. This is known as a 'crossed' transaction.

A crossed transaction is also where a conversation is initiated by an ego, but the response received by the other ego, is different to what you were expecting. Even if you receive the expected ego, the expected response is different.

If a crossed transaction occurs, you must immediately shift your ego to either an adult, or to the same ego as your respondent. Remember that if the responding ego is a child and you choose to change your ego to a child, the result will be conflict. As a general rule, you are best to take on the adult ego in this situation.

Taking on the parent ego does not integrate well with this theory. If an immature child has responded to your conversation stimulus, then the last thing they are looking for is parenting advice. This will not only open a potential second avenue to conflict, but you will lose control of the conversation. It will generally end at that point or the child respondent will continue to be childish. If you engage in conflict, whether as a parent or a child ego, the control of the conversation is lost. It is important you become an adult.

Looking at the earlier example, you again receive a response from a child ego. Instead of receiving the expected response of a scared ego, you receive the immature response of, "Whatever you reckon! I will do what I like before a game!".

A crossed transaction has occurred, so you must initiate the adult ego to avoid conflict. If you use the parent ego and respond with authority, you will likely engage conflict. Even if you apply nurture or sympathy to your response, this reaction will undermine the child and again, likely start conflict.

The only solution here is to become an adult. After analysing your parent and child roots and the data you have gathered as an adult, you respond with, "Okay. If you want to drink alcohol before a game, that is up to you. But if your performance is not up to the standard I expect, don't be offended if your drinking is used against you".

In this situation, you have responded as an adult and likely ended the conversation in complete control. You have re-affirmed your initial parent ego by responding to a child ego as an adult. You have successfully overcome a crossed transaction.

Ulterior Transactions

To confuse matters further, you may initiate conversation or respond by saying one thing, where your goal is to deliver a message different from what you physically said. It is this message that is picked up by the other party, not the words. This is known as an 'ulterior' transaction.

An ulterior transaction is once again a conversation initiated by an ego, but the response received by the other ego, is different to what you were expecting. Even if you receive the expected ego, the expected response is different. To complete the transaction, you respond with an ego that has an ulterior motive to the words you use.

Returning to the drinking example, you respond to the child ego with your own child ego by saying, "Fine. Drink as much as you want".

It is probable that you have lost control of the conversation by delivering your ulterior transaction. You may have actually said to keep drinking, but your ulterior motive is to deliver the original message on the same level as the child. You are attempting to get your point across by dropping to the same level as your respondent. As you learnt earlier, Child vs Child transactions result in conflict. Your attempt at an ulterior message in this instance, has lost you control of the conversation.

You can use ulterior transactions with an adult ego, but my advice would be to tread carefully. My belief is that ulterior messages create distrust within your team and such deceit can result in internal destruction of team culture. Ulterior discussions can confuse team-mates and spoil team goal congruence. You may lose the respect of your comrades and in that instance, you have lost control. You will have no option but to stand down or move on.

In summary, this section may be long-winded and heavily detailed, but gaining a knowledge and understanding for transactions and egos will help you communicate better moving forward. You must be clear on how to avoid conversational conflict, and if such conflict arises, trigger your adult ego to either end or regain control of the conversation.

If there is anything I have learnt about conversation in my lifetime, it is to always tell the truth. As an adult ego, the truth may temporarily offend or disgruntle somebody, but ultimately, they will respect you in the long run. White lies, little fibs, childish behaviour, or ulterior transactions will all come back to haunt you eventually. Swallow your pride and take the short-term pain.

Once you have gained the trust of your team-mates, your conversation will always involve implied respect. With this respect, it is likely that every word that comes out of your mouth will be taken on board with gratitude and treated as gospel. You will not only have control of conversation, but an influence on the way your team acts, behaves, and performs.

CHAPTER 12

Human Nature

Human nature is defined as the general psychological characteristics, feelings, and behavioural traits of humankind, shared by all humans. Human nature is said to be the natural way all humans think, act, and react.

The idea of human nature has been debated for many centuries. There have been numerous theories supporting the existence of human nature, but just as many debunking the whole concept.

On one hand you have studies analysing human nature, promoting its genetic inheritance for all who exist, while on the other hand, there are opposing ideals that human nature does not exist, and that emotions, behaviours, actions, and reactions, are all instilled in us from an early age.

My research on human nature has given me more questions than answers. Does human nature really exist? Are we born with a genetic make-up that means we must think, act, and feel a certain way? Or does our childhood and later learnings set the foundation of our emotions and behaviour? I accepted arguments and opinions from both sides of the fence but was unable to commit totally to either side.

Rather than go into detail about ancient philosophy, modern philosophy, Christian theology, or the scientific viewpoint, I feel it more appropriate to discuss human nature in its most simple form. After assessing many published studies on human nature, I conclude the following:
   1) Human nature has nothing to do with nature itself
   2) Human nature decides how you feel, but not how you act or react
   3) Mental illness may affect how you feel, act, or react

Human nature has nothing to do with nature itself

The term human nature is related purely to the common trends of the way humans live their lives or are expected to live their lives. In no way does this terminology relate to nature itself.

The law of attraction states that it is impossible to become a separate-self, and that a human must be at one with nature. This does not mean a human has to be at one with human nature. This distinction is important as the first law of attraction (like attracts like) implies that human thoughts, actions, and reactions can be changed, depending on what we attract. A thought may surface naturally in any given situation. The thought can be believed, ignored, modified, or eliminated depending on how you choose act or react.

Human Nature decides how you feel but, not how you act or react

Every human being has seven basic needs:
- Biological and Physiological needs
- Cognitive needs
- Esteem needs
- Love needs
- Aesthetic needs
- Safety needs
- Self-actualisation needs

Common natural thoughts exist throughout all humanity in relation to these seven basic needs. If any of these needs are not provided or are challenged, then a natural thought will surface.

As an example, a human must drink water to survive. A natural biological thought may be, "I'm thirsty and should get some water". Whether you act on that natural thought and get the water, is purely up to you. You could continue playing your match and decide to delay getting it. You could also ask someone else to get the water for you. You could even dismiss the thought completely and not drink any water at all.

Another example could be while playing in a match. Your opponent plays an amazing bowl and gets the shot while you were holding a large count. In this situation, your esteem needs are challenged, and you have the natural thought of, "That shot really makes me angry". How you react to that natural thought is once again up to you. You could show a burst of anger and let out your frustration. You could apply an anger management technique to calm yourself down. You could even give your opponent a high-five and congratulate them on a great shot.

My key point is that human nature decides how you feel in certain situations. This is a natural response to one of the seven basic needs. How you feel does not necessarily mean how you will act or react. Human nature may make you feel like you want to act or react in a certain way, but how you actually react is up to you; it is your choice. A thought, whether natural or not, is only a thought. Human nature does not decide what you choose to do with that thought. You can believe it, ignore it, change it, or eliminate it.

You need to understand this valuable point about human nature. You must be clear that certain feelings and thoughts are natural and that this is okay. How you deal with those thoughts characterise your level of mental toughness. The whole concept of this book is to deliver the message that human nature may make you think or feel a certain way, but you decide how to act or react.

You may let thoughts control your emotions and behaviour from time to time. So long as you learn from the situation and develop your experience, you are more likely to act or react better in the same position next time. There may be many champions in bowls, but only a true champion knows how to act or react to natural thoughts.

Mental illness may affect how you feel, act, or react

Mental illnesses such as depression, anxiety disorder, schizophrenia, obsessive compulsive disorder, autism, and bipolar disorder, just to name a few, may all have a direct impact on how you feel, act, or react.

If you have a mental illness, you can experience both natural and unnatural thoughts, where such thoughts can result in unhealthy emotional and behavioural responses. Teaching yourself mental toughness can help re-program the way you deal with thoughts and feelings. Coupled with professional treatment, mental toughness can not only improve your level of enjoyment in sport, but your day-to-day life too. I am a proven triumph of this combination.

If you are coaching or mentoring someone with a mental disability, be sure you understand their condition before imposing new tasks and responsibilities. It is not impossible for them to learn mental toughness, but some barriers may be extremely difficult to break down. Giving them something to take home and read is better than trying to explain your intentions face to face. Often, you are best to focus on physical attributes like their bowls delivery and leave mental interaction to the medical professionals.

PART C

Attitude

CHAPTER 13

Internal Dialogue

Internal dialogue is your internal talk. It is the voice inside your head that nobody else hears other than you.

Famous American Doctor Phil McGraw has been quoted on internal dialogue saying, "What you say inside your head can make or break your life". This commentary sets the path for your beliefs, emotions, and actions. In other words, your attitude.

If you believe the world is 'such and such' then it will be 'such and such' If you believe it to be 'so and so' then it will be 'so and so'.

Your internal dialogue proposes a path for how you act. It exists while working, reading, watching television, eating, playing sport and every other possible scenario in life. It even exists while you are asleep.

Your internal dialogue will provide a running commentary of your life. It will judge people, comment on an event occurring or one about to happen and even procrastinate. It can be dominatingly aggressive, but also destructive.

Internal dialogue can be both negative and positive. Such dialogue can create a snowball effect, where the more you think about something, the more probable it will become real.

Your internal dialogue can stir emotions, use up your energy and attach you to any given thought.

In lawn bowls, there are many situations during a game where your internal dialogue is relevant. It will continually talk to you at all stages of a match. When you are behind or playing poorly, negative thoughts can doubt your ability to succeed. On the other hand, a positive dialogue leads you to perseverant and supreme confidence and feeds your extrinsic motivation.

Almost everyone knows that a voice exists inside their head. Sometimes you are not aware it is even talking to you until you are reminded that it is there. You have both conscious and subconscious internal dialogue.

This section of the book gives insight on self-belief, positive thinking, eliminating negative thoughts and body language.

If you have a predictable and positive internal dialogue, your mental toughness will greatly benefit from these subjects.

Your internal dialogue can become positively predictable once you are clear with the critical theories of mental toughness, discussed earlier in this book.

Victim theory and the empowerment dynamic give an understanding that you must act as a creator and not a victim. Once a victim, your internal dialogue automatically become negative, limiting the chances of achieving set goals and desired results. As a creator, you truly believe that your challenger is merely a bump in the road on the avenue to success and your focus remains positive.

The law of attraction tells you that 'like attracts like', so the way you talk to yourself can set the basis for what is to happen. A healthy internal dialogue is likely to attract healthy outcomes. If your internal dialogue is unhealthy, it is likely to attract unhealthy outcomes.

If conditioning determines your attitude and behaviour, then you can condition your internal dialogue. You might not be able to observe the internal dialogue of others, but you can certainly introduce classical or operant strategies to improve your internal dialogue.

Courage tells you that it is okay to have fears so long as you confront them. Your internal dialogue will attempt to place barriers between you and your fears and to block you from demonstrating courage. This is your survival instinct. A developed phobia may make it almost impossible to confront your fears, however this is unlikely on a bowling green. Courage is used to overcome nerves and the fear of failure and you need your internal dialogue to be courageous.

Altering your internal dialogue is a willpower choice. You decide whether you want to do something about your thoughts or not. If unwanted thoughts exist, you must make the decision to eliminate them and replace them with wanted thoughts. At times, your internal dialogue may release a message on impulse, but you must stop, assess, and make a mindful choice.

Your internal dialogue must also be aware of the established theories of mental toughness. This knowledge will ensure awareness of other factors that directly impact what you are thinking (or are supposed to be thinking).

Over time, your experience on internal dialogue will develop. Do not be afraid to have an unhealthy thought, this is only natural. However, your experience will only grow when you gain the ability to identify the unhealthy thought, assess the thought, and finally alter the thought, before taking any action.

Your level of confidence can jump from acceptance, perseverance or supreme purely based on what your conscience is saying. Already, you know that confidence must never slip to the acceptance level and thus, your internal dialogue needs to enforce a 'never give up' attitude.

Your motivation to achieve can be influenced by powerful negative thoughts, that doubt your ability to reach set goals and desired results. This lack of self-belief is caused by a toxic internal dialogue. Motivation should always exist, even if negative thoughts arise. You still want to win, but this distracting, sour, internal dialogue interferes and the focus on your goals is lost.

Internal dialogue may attract you to the cognitive illusion of momentum, veering you away from your game plan and limiting your chances of gaining a desired result. You have already learnt that so-called momentum, is simply the ups and downs of a match and it should not influence your game plan or the decisions you make. The word 'momentum' must never appear in your internal dialogue.

During a conversation, your internal dialogue will encourage you to say what you are thinking. Always remember to stop, assess the opposing ego, and ensure you respond as an adult. The process of thinking before you speak has never been so important.

Practical Internal Dialogue Exercise

If you are unsure of the general condition of your thoughts and internal dialogue, there is a simple exercise you can undertake.

Take a pen and small notepad and place it in your pocket at the start of a day. Every time you have a thought or hear your conscience speak, write it down. Before you go to bed, separate the thoughts into negative and positive.

Those who do the exercise properly will have at least 100 statements. More than half of these thoughts will be negative. It is human nature to be pessimistic and negative, worrying about many things that challenge your seven basic needs.

From the list, accentuate the positives and eliminate the negatives. Read the positive internal dialogue at least twice over and ensure you cross out any negative dialogue. This process is repeated daily until the number of negative thoughts in a day make up 25% of dialogue or less.

Part of completing this exercise constructively is to be honest with yourself. You must write down all internal dialogue and not just pick and choose what to put on paper. Leaving out negative dialogue defeats the purpose of the exercise, impacting the likely effectiveness of the process. The list is for your eyes only so don't be afraid of what you record, just take pleasure in scribbling out the negatives and reaffirming the positives each night.

Over time, you will be able to remove negative dialogue as it arises and replace it with positive dialogue. It won't happen overnight, but if you decide you want to improve your thoughts and internal dialogue, this exercise is proven to work. I have done it myself.

CHAPTER 14

Self-Belief

Self-belief or self-confidence is an attitude choice that relates specifically to self-assurance in your own judgment, ability, and power.

If self-belief is an attitude choice, then your personal level of self-belief is not set in stone. When making the conscious willpower choice to improve your self-belief, you create an opportunity to become not only a better bowler, but a better person in everyday life.

Without self-belief, you have nothing. A failure to achieve self-belief in life will leave you lonely, depressed, regretful, disappointed, and often a victim of the world itself.

It took me many years to find self-belief. I had to learn to love myself despite mental illness, self-doubts, limited opportunity, and a string of regrets and failures.

Despite all the battles of daily life and the difficult situations that may arise, self-belief will define your character, help you overcome fear and create an internal relationship with yourself. If 'like attracts like' then a positive attitude will encourage self-belief, while a pessimistic attitude will open the door to self-doubt.

Self-belief is a God-given right that exists within everyone. The key is learning how to activate it and use it to your advantage on the bowling green.

Eleanor Roosevelt once said that, "Nobody can make you feel inferior without your consent". If you have true belief in yourself, your ability, and your goals, then any negativity expressed by others about you, should be dismissed. Only when we consent to listening and accepting the negativity, can it make us feel inferior. So, ignore it.

I have undergone many hours of self-belief research and have developed a five-step guide on developing your self-belief.

1) <u>You can learn self-belief</u>
Self-belief can be taught and learnt. Your current level of self-belief does not have to remain at the same level forever. You

need to discard ideas that limit yourself from achieving your overall goals and re-affirm self-confidence.

As an example, playing a high-quality opponent in lawn bowls may give you reason to doubt your self-belief. You should not limit yourself on what you can achieve in the match.

Saying you would be happy to achieve a certain number of shots provides a limit to what you believe you can achieve. You should discard any such thoughts and affirm self-confidence in executing your game plan to the best of your ability.

If you are not distracted by limiting thoughts and are constantly affirming self-confidence, then who knows what you could achieve in the match? Your opponent may be distracted or intimidated by your positive attitude, relying on you to fold easier than expected. This self-belief could ultimately transfer to the scoreboard, resulting in a victory.

2) Be your own mind coach

Victim Theory taught you the ability to avoid falling victim to a persecutor and to become a creator facing a challenger. The theory also explained that in the empowerment dynamic, it was possible for a creator to be their own coach. To develop your self-belief, you should attempt to be your own mind coach.

When you doubt yourself, there should be instant alarm bells ringing in your head. Any arisen doubt should automatically trigger the coach.

As your own mind coach, you should be slapping quotes at yourself like, "Why are you doubting yourself? You can do this!" and "You played a similar shot four ends ago in this direction, on that hand. You know where the line and weight are, so go and get it".

The coach is the level head that removes doubts, affirms the positive and reinforces the ideas of the creator and the empowerment dynamic. You can have a two-way internal conversation between your doubting conscience and the clear thinking, straight-talking coach. Your conscience may give rise to a child ego from time to time, but your mind coach will influence the conversation as an adult. Instead of falling victim and seeking a rescuer, the adult coach will control the conversation and ensure that your internal dialogue reaffirms self-belief, forcing your conscience once again to take on the role of a creator.

3) <u>Find a mentor</u>
A mentor is someone you look up to and try to emulate. You can learn from the way they act and behave, their grace under pressure and the characteristics that make them successful. Finding a mentor is a method of observational conditioning, where their attitude and self-belief is on show for all to see.

In lawn bowls, there are many people who have mentors. Mentors can provide assurance that you too can be successful no matter who you are, or where you come from.

When you find a mentor, you will discover that they are a normal human being just like you. They too experience self-doubts and negative thoughts from time to time and have their very own way of developing self-belief.

You can learn many things from your mentor, including tips on self-belief. As self-belief is an attitude choice, you too can make decisions on the kind of self-confidence you wish to take forward.

Great mentors are not always the most elite bowlers. They may be a person from another sport, your coach or even a parent. All that matters is that you idolise someone and believe that you can not only achieve what they have done, but that you can do even better. One day you might become a mentor yourself.

Self-belief can develop from the presence of a mentor, freshen your extrinsic motivation, and increase your chances of achieving goals and desired results.

4) Failure is an option

Never be afraid of failure. Failure will often teach you a valuable lesson, expand your experience and increase the probability of achieving next time around.

You must understand that failure is an option. The only true failure is not attempting something in the first place.

When you overcome the fear of failure, you give yourself a greater opportunity to succeed. Even the great bowlers do not win every event they enter but by entering all the events possible, they increase their chances of winning multiple titles. Every time you experience the thrill of a win or a title, your self-belief grows.

Later in this book I discuss how to deal with success and failure. In short, you must learn to brush aside failures after review, and to celebrate your victories. If you can flood your mind with thoughts of victory and success, there is little or no room left to focus on failures and defeats.

5) Powerful Self-Visualisation

Of the five steps in this model, I judge powerful self-visualisation as the most beneficial. You can condition yourself to a higher level of self-belief and self-confidence. It involves a daily exercise that is married to the law of attraction.

Find a quiet place where you can sit, undisturbed for a minimum of five minutes. Sit down, make yourself comfortable and close your eyes.

Picture yourself achieving one of your long-term goals. Take the time to imagine how it feels to achieve that ultimate success. Once you feel at one with the success, picture yourself in the sky, watching from above. Take mental images, note your emotions, surroundings, and overwhelming pride. An epiphany of awesomeness.

The more you picture yourself achieving your goals and the more positively you think about them, the greater your chances of achieving them. When you are ultimately in that position for real, you have already visualised the outcome. From there, you know to achieve that desired result, all you must do is understand the processes ahead and follow your routine. If the law of attraction is real, and 'like really does attract like', then the result will take care of itself.

As well as the five-step model, there is another simple tip that may help develop your self-belief. It is verbal affirmation that positively predicts the future. Something as simple as waking up every day and saying out aloud that "Today is going to be a great day", or before a match, saying aloud that "This is going to be a great match", can give you the self-belief that it actually will be. Call it 'mirage self-belief' if you like, but as we learnt earlier with confidence, the act of pretending can trick yourself into believing something is real. Again, 'like attracts like'.

Even if you are pessimistic about this simple tip or the five-step guide to developing self-belief, I encourage you to at least give it a go. On the chance that it works, you will not only develop a stronger self-confidence in bowls but improve your self-belief in everyday life. It has certainly worked for me.

CHAPTER 15

Positive Thinking

As with self-belief, positive thinking is an attitude choice. Positive thinking is a mental and emotional attitude that forces you to focus on the good things. The power to think positively encourages the expectation of positive results and outcomes.

As a positive thinker you understand you are a creator, not a victim. You understand that although negative thoughts may arise from time to time, they can be eliminated and replaced with positive thoughts.

If you think positively, you will attract positivity. The law of attraction applies to positive thinking. If 'like attracts like', then positive thoughts encourage the attraction of positive responses and outcomes and if your thoughts are not perfect, then you need to try and perfect the thoughts you are having.

As positive thinking is an attitude choice, you can condition yourself to become a positive thinker. Apply the classical approach and pair a song or some music to a positive thought. You could instrumentally reward yourself for a string of positive thoughts, while penalising yourself anytime negativity controls your thought pattern. Further, you could observe the positivity of a mentor, stimulating positivity within yourself. Conditioning can teach you to become a more positive thinker.

Nerves and self-doubt block your ability to think positively. You need to face these fears and find the courage to overcome them. Only then, is your mind free to think positive again.

For positive thinking to exist in your game of bowls, it needs to be adopted into your everyday life. Positive thinking is a total attitude shift, that cannot just be turned on or off at will. You not only need to be aware of the existence of positive thinking and how it relates to the critical theories of mental toughness, but you need to integrate it in every single thing you do.

Having a positive attitude allows you to experience positive realities; brightness is added to your eyes, there is a lift in your energy level, and you feel a noticeable increase in happiness. Your positive attitude produces an aura that expands to the people around you. It can be contagious.

So how do you develop your positive thinking?

As with self-belief, I have identified a five-step guide on how to develop your positive thinking.

1) Smile

No matter how hard things get or however many negative thoughts attempt to overwhelm you, just smile! Smiling is not only proven to boost your mood, it helps your body release endorphins that reduce pain, blood pressure and stress. A reduction in stress has a direct correlation with how you think. Reduced stress will relax your mind and invite a surge of positive thoughts, eliminating and taking the place of all negativity.

2) Language

Use words like 'yes', 'can', 'will' and 'definitely'. These words are known to have a positive influence on yourself and others. Avoid words like 'no', 'can't', 'won't' and 'maybe'. These words are known to have a negative influence on yourself and others.

As an example, you might be asked by a friend to meet for dinner that night, but you have other plans. Instead of answering 'no' to the question and protruding negativity, answer with a positive response such as 'I can definitely be available for dinner on Friday'. This positive response solves both problems i.e. you are not available that night, even if you wanted to go for dinner, and your friend still gets to catch up with you later in the week.

3) Avoid Negative People

Surrounding yourself with negative people will induce your own personal negativity. You need to evade all negative and toxic people, or risk losing your own positive attractiveness. To think positively, you must involve yourself with positive people, or at least encourage positivity from the negative people.

4) Replace negative thoughts

You cannot eliminate a negative thought unless you replace it with a positive thought. If the thought you are having is not perfect, then we need to perfect it. The most practical way of doing so, is to identify the negative thought, acknowledge it for what it is and replace it with a positive thought. Negative thoughts are destructive and must be replaced by positive thoughts immediately. We discuss the elimination of negative thoughts in more detail in the next chapter.

5) Powerful Self-Visualisation

As with self-belief, the most beneficial and powerful way to develop your positive thinking, is through self-visualisation. Without sounding repetitive, powerful self-visualisation is linked with the law of attraction and can be practiced daily.

Find a quiet place where you can sit, undisturbed for a minimum of five minutes. Sit down, make yourself comfortable and close your eyes.

Picture yourself winning a club championship singles. Take the time to imagine what it feels like to become a club singles champion. Once you feel at one with the success, picture yourself watching from above. Take mental images and note your emotions, surroundings, and overwhelming pride.

The more you picture yourself achieving success and the more positively you think about it, the greater your chances of it becoming a reality. Next time you are in the club singles final, you have already visualised the outcome. From there, you know to achieve that desired result, all you must do is understand the processes ahead and follow your routine. If the law of attraction is real, and 'like really does attract like', then the result will take care of itself. Positive thinking goes from revelation to reality.

Positive thoughts are not natural. By adopting this five-step model, your overall level of positivity is bound to increase. Over time, positive thinking will become part of your character, naturalising the concept within you. Positive thinking will automatically occur subconsciously as a habit, rather than a chore. You will no longer need to acknowledge negative thoughts, as you have already eliminated them, or they no longer exist.

Positive thinking truly is a powerful tool that if used to your maximum potential, can yield consistent and regular success. Knowing the broad lack of positivity among many lawn bowlers, your positive attitude could mean the difference between winning and losing. That declaration alone should provide you with enough motivation to at least give it a go.

CHAPTER 16

Eliminating Negative Thoughts

Negative thoughts program your mind to focus on the things that can, and will, go wrong. Fear, anxiety, worry, and negative thinking are not only counter-productive, but they drain your energy.

It is almost impossible to go through your daily life without negative thoughts popping into your head from time to time. The important thing is to identify the thought, acknowledge it for what it is and then replace with a positive thought. Eliminating negative thoughts is an attitude choice.

When thinking negatively, you are more likely to avoid being a creator, and take on the role of a victim. Negative thoughts will arise from time to time and instead of treating them as a challenger and using the coach, you rely on a rescuer. A negative thinker lives in the drama triangle, so without immediate action, they will be unable to use the empowerment dynamic.

If you think negatively, you will attract negativity. The law of attraction applies to negative thinking. If 'like attracts like', then negative thoughts encourage the attraction of negative responses and outcomes, and if your thoughts are not perfect, you need to try and perfect the thoughts you already have.

As eliminating negative thoughts is an attitude choice, you can condition yourself to remove any unhealthy internal dialogue. As discussed in the positive thinking section, you can apply the classical approach by pairing positive thoughts to some music. If a negative thought appears, identify it, acknowledge it for what it is, distract yourself with the music and introduce a positive replacement. You could instrumentally penalise yourself for thinking negatively, while rewarding yourself for a string of positive thoughts. You can even observe the positivity of your team-mates or opposition, using that positivity to stimulate yourself. Conditioning can help you to eliminate negative thoughts.

Negative thinking impedes our ability to think positively. Such thinking encourages disappointment, anger, frustration, and excuses to dismiss the game plan. You need the courage to overcome negative thoughts by identifying them, acknowledging them for what they are and replacing them with positive thoughts. It takes courage to go directly against your internal dialogue.

I have come up with four techniques to eliminate negative thoughts. For some bowlers, one technique is enough to improve their thought pattern. Other bowlers may need to use multiple techniques. I have used all four methods over time with the first being a clear favourite. The key is to use what works for you.

1) <u>Recognise and distract</u>
Negative thoughts are only a thought. The only power they hold over you, is the power you choose to give them. When a negative thought arrives, seek a distraction that is positive. The distraction will replace the negative thought with a positive. Now that the positive exists, re-focus on the game and exchange that positive to something more relevant. This is classical conditioning.

As an example, you may play a bowl that gives the shot away. With only one bowl left to play, you fear the end is probably lost. You need to identify the thought as negative, acknowledge it for what it is and seek a distraction. Through classical conditioning, you pair a piece of music with a positive thought. Now that the negative has been eliminated, you can re-focus on the game. The new positive feeling allows you to exchange that positive thought with a more relevant positive thought. You no longer think about giving the shot away, but begin planning how you will get it back with your last bowl.

2) Change the thought to positive

Although simple in theory, directly changing your thoughts from negative to positive is probably the hardest technique to master. Some bowlers have the ability to stay positive most of the time, not allowing negative thoughts to surface. As their attitude is generally positive, negative thoughts are easier to eliminate and replace.

Many young bowlers play with extraordinary energy, without the fear of failure. This relaxed, free-flowing and high tempo style leaves so little time to think, that negative thoughts have little chance of surviving. This attitude is risk/reward and can bring inconsistent results, but outcomes that cannot be blamed on negativity.

Bowlers with a history of yoga and meditation have more chance of using this method to eliminate negative thoughts. The mind must have some sort of base training to use it effectively. This technique is more valuable once you have conquered self-belief and positive thinking.

3) Relax with humour

Negative thoughts make the body tense, increase your heart rate, and create a stressed mindset. To relax your body, you can use humour.

If humour makes you smile or chuckle, your blood pressure lowers, stress reduces, and pain is extinguished. The thought of something funny or even cracking a joke can bring on a smile or laughter. You don't have to make the joke out aloud; it can be an internal thought. A nervous smile is better than storing anger and frustration.

You have learnt that smiling is a way of inviting positive thoughts, so relaxing with humour can not only eliminate negatives, but make room for positivity.

4) <u>Repetition and affirmation</u>
When a negative thought arrives, you need to re-affirm a positive situation or outcome and repeat it over and over again. Think about a good shot you played earlier in the match, or a moment in the game when your confidence was supreme. This positive repetition and affirmation will overwhelm the negative thought and force your mind to surrender to positivity.

Negative thoughts can appear at any time in a match, even when you are in front on the scoreboard. You can avoid most of them by constantly accentuating earlier positives and repeating them throughout the remainder of the match.

By learning these techniques, you can make positivity a habit. Continually identifying negatives, acknowledging them for what they are and eliminating them, is all part of conditioning your attitude. Although almost impossible to remove all negativity from your game, you now have a framework to deal with negative thoughts.

Such skilful thinking will improve your overall attitude on the green.

CHAPTER 17

Body Language

Body language is the non-verbal communication you express, that can be read by the people around you. Body language can be consciously performed or can be triggered subconsciously.

Body language is everything from a gesture or wave, right through to facial expression and eye movement. Every movement your body makes gives away clues of how you are feeling internally.

Have you ever played a poor bowl and seen your skipper throw their hands in the air and turn their back? Although they haven't actually said anything out aloud, their poor body language gives you complete understanding of how they are feeling.

This chapter deals with both positive and negative body language. It will also teach you how to read the body language of your team-mates and opponents. If you can master the skill of body language analysis, you will be able to read the feelings and internal emotions of those around you. You will also learn how your body language can affect the performance of team-mates and opponents. Displaying negative body language will not only drop the shoulders of your comrades, but potentially lift the spirit of your opposition.

Body language can be obvious, like the cranky and upset skipper example above. However, a lot of body language is not so obvious. To the untrained eye, body language can be difficult to identify and impossible to analyse.

Developing analytical skills in this area will prompt you to take care of disheartened team-mates. Sometimes a team-mate may be down or unwell, but not showing any of the clear signs. You could be the reason for lifting their performance or spirits and making sure they become a valuable contributor in the match.

Picking up on negative body language by your opponent could inspire you to put the foot down and 'go for the kill'. You may be only one or two blows away from getting them to their knees. This is the perfect time to demonstrate your own positive body language, lift your energy and make every shot a winner.

It can be difficult to trust an opponent on the bowling green, especially if you are not friendly off the green. During a match, you need to treat your opponent with scepticism. Keeping a closer eye on their actions rather than their verbal communication, will give you a better idea of how they are feeling. People lie on the green. They often provide false and misleading information hoping that you will 'bite' and take it onboard. Accepting this information will distract you from your game plan and potentially confuse your mental stability. If you want to know exactly how your opponent is really feeling, watch their body language.

As a guide, you should never take any advice from an opponent during the match. If you want advice or help, the best time to ask is after the game. Most opponents will be happy to discuss the game and any questions you may have, especially if you are a new bowler or an inexperienced bowler.

When you pick up that an opponent is showing negative body language, you become aware that they are under pressure, feeling disinterested, worried, scared or a mixture of all. If you see negative body language within your own team, you need to address it immediately. In any event, it is important you understand all types of body language; from the obvious to the secretive.

Positive Body Language

Examples of obvious positive body language include:
- Clapping
- Pumped fist
- Acknowledgment to the crowd or team-mates
- Nodding
- Jumping
- Jogging or running
- Smiling
- One arm in the air with the index finger raised
- Patting a team mate on the back

Other positive body language which is not so obvious includes:
- Winking
- One hand on the chin
- Direct eye contact
- Stretching, especially when stretching the arms over your head with fingers interlocked
- Standing up when given the option to sit down
- Standing with feet a comfortable distance apart
- Rubbing hands together

The above two lists give you a broad range of positive body language, but it is not exhaustive; you could add many more. The first list provides the most obvious displays which can generally be picked up by all bowlers. The second list gives examples of subtle positivity that most are unaware of. It is also a list that you can practice as a way of developing your own positive body language.

Demonstrating positive body language shows your team that you are a creator, not a victim. You and your team understand that negative body language can creep in from time to time but are also aware that the role of a coach can correct it.

If you demonstrate positive body language, you will attract positivity. The law of attraction applies to positive body language. If 'like attracts like', then positive body language can encourage the attraction of positive responses, outcomes, and vibes. If your body language is not perfect, then you need to perfect the body language you already have.

As positive body language is an attitude choice, you can condition yourself to demonstrate higher positivity. You can instrumentally reward yourself for a string of positive body language, while penalising yourself anytime your body language is negative. Further, you could observe the positive body language of a mentor, stimulating positivity within yourself. Conditioning can help develop positive body language.

Nerves and self-doubt affect your body language. You need to face these fears and find the courage to overcome them. Only then, is your mind free to demonstrate positive body language again.

Negative Body Language

Examples of obvious negative body language on the bowling green include:
- Kicking the ground
- Throwing a mat
- Facing the ground or looking down, whether being spoken to or not
- Frowning
- Crossing arms
- Turning away from a situation
- Rolling the eyes
- Biting nails
- Hands in pockets
- Stamping feet
- Moping when walking
- Hands on head

Other negative body language which is not so obvious include:
- Scratching
- Rubbing the nose
- Blinking for a time longer than normal
- Breathing in out aloud
- Tensed lips
- Gritting teeth
- Rushing
- Chewing gum faster or smoking more regularly
- Standing with feet close together

The above two lists give you a broad range of negative body language. The first list provides the clearest negativity which can generally be picked up by everyone. The second list explores ideas that many bowlers are completely unaware of. This subtle body language may not be so obvious, but they are signs that your opponent or your team-mate is experiencing negative thoughts.

Next time you go to your bowling club, sit-down and watch a match from the sideline. See if you can identify the subtle signs of negativity and timely compare them to the head position or the scoreboard. Suddenly, you will become alert of every move a bowler makes, and the indistinct signs of negative body language become far more obvious.

On a personal level, you must try to avoid negative body language as much as possible on the green. There will be times when you slip up, so don't beat yourself up over it. As with a negative thought, you can identify the negative body language, acknowledge it for what it is and eliminate it.

Body language is especially important in singles, as there is normally minimal verbal communication or noise during a singles match. The score will not always dictate the internal feelings of both players. Be aware of your opponent's body language. Should they provide negative signs, step on the gas, and take full advantage. If you make the most of their negativity, it can often find its way to the scoreboard. In a close match, this could be the difference between winning and losing.

An intelligent bowler will feed ferociously off any negative body language. They will use every possible angle to gain an advantage in a match.

As with confidence and self-belief, negative body language can be turned around by producing a mirage. You can apply 'mirage positive body language' by acting positive, even when you are having negative thoughts. Your team-mates and your opponent may have no idea you are experiencing negativity if you refuse to show anything that isn't positive.

For example, if you feel nervous, tense, or frustrated, apply one of the positive body language techniques immediately. Even if you feel completely negative in that moment, producing positive body language will give the impression that you are fine. If 'like attracts like' then the act of mirage positive body language could internally produce more positive thoughts and feelings. You can literally trick yourself into a fresh, positive frame of mind.

CHAPTER 18

Concentration

Concentration is defined as the action or power of focusing your attention.

Former Australian test cricketer Ian Healy has stated that, "the average human gets approximately one hour of concentration per day". As a wicketkeeper there are times where he would have fielded for six hours or more in one day. This sort of time frame can be compared to a long day on the bowling green.

If Ian Healy is right, how is it possible for a lawn bowler to concentrate for an entire match, or further still, multiple matches in one day? Quite frankly, it is impossible.

The average lawn bowler is inefficient with their concentration. Their concentration is often lost after the first 10 ends of play, inefficiently used up and wasted.

Efficient use of concentration takes experience and skill. There are many times during a match when you do not have to concentrate on what is happening. Even when skipping, the concentration required for calling each shot may only be 10 seconds at a time. When bowling yourself, you will only need around 10-15 seconds per bowl delivered. You must express interest in the game at all other times, but do not need to specifically concentrate.

I have some great tips on how to improve your concentration levels. There are many short-term solutions that may assist at a specific time, but ultimately, we want to develop and expand your concentration levels permanently.

If you have exceptional concentration you will always act as a creator, not a victim. You understand that although lapses in concentration may arise from time to time, the role of a coach can correct it.

Developing your concentration is an attitude choice. You can condition yourself to concentrate. Apply the classical approach and pair a physical action with your concentration. I like to click my fingers whenever I feel distracted. This action makes me concentrate instantly. You could also observe the concentration of a mentor, taking mental notes on how and when they flick the concentration switch. Conditioning can improve your concentration efficiency.

Nerves and self-doubt waste your concentration. You need to face these fears and find the courage to overcome them. Without nerves, you can allocate your concentration more efficiently over the course of a day.

Examples of short-term solutions or 'quick-fixes' for concentration include caffeine and sugar. These may give you a sense of energy and uplift for short periods but do nothing to increase concentration longevity moving forward.

Developing Long-Term Concentration

The best method to improve your concentration longevity is to eradicate procrastination. Constantly thinking about tasks or jobs you need to do is absolutely exhausting, and a pure waste of concentration. Instead of thinking about doing something for hours on end, acknowledge the task and complete it. If you don't have the time to do it right away, make a plan for when you can complete it later on. At least this way, you will stop thinking about it.

Exercise is a great way to stimulate concentration. There have been many studies on the benefits of exercise and fitness and its connection with concentration. Amazingly, aerobic exercise has been discovered as the best form of exercise to increase concentration levels. It is believed that exercise triggers the release of certain chemicals in the brain that improve immediate and long-term functioning of concentration and attention.

Hydration is one of the easiest ways to improve your concentration level. You are always hearing people telling you to drink plenty of water, especially when playing bowls. The idea is straight-forward, but one that many bowlers ignore. Once you become thirsty, you are already in the early stages of dehydration. Caffeine and alcohol contribute highly to dehydration and water is required to dilute the effects of both. If you don't visit the bathroom at least once in a match, you are probably not drinking enough fluids.

A solid sleeping pattern will do wonders for your concentration. If your body clock is used to feeling tired at a specific time of the night, and used to feeling wide awake at a specific time in the morning, then chances are that your alertness and concentration will be more productive during the day. Having a regular bed-time will help establish a consistent body clock.

Finally, the simple act of wiggling your fingers or toes can snap you out of an absentminded state. When identifying a slip in concentration, a quick wiggle of your fingers or toes can revive your concentration.

Focus

Focus is the centre of your interest or activity.

There are points in a match where absolute focus is required. Often your instinct or 'gut feel' identifies an important shot, a big end, or a critical moment in the match. This is where you apply focus and block absolutely everything else out, attempting to seize the moment.

Focus absorbs your concentration levels, where over-using focus can leave you exhausted part-way through a match. Experience will help you identify the right time to apply focus.

PART D

Planning

CHAPTER 19

SMART Goals

Without goals, you have no direction. It is possible to reach a certain level in bowls, and due to lack of goals and direction, you plateau. Your form may ebb and flow, but you will not improve.

By setting goals, you provide yourself with guidance on what you want to achieve. Although you may not succeed all the time, your extrinsic motivation will guarantee improvement in your overall game. Goals make you strive to become better.

All bowlers should have a list of short-term, mid-term and long-term goals.

Short-Term Goals
Short-term goals or desired results are goals you set to achieve in the next moment, hour, day, week and month. You do not

need to write all your short-term goals down on paper, as most of them occur by the minute. As an example, choosing a shot to play in a match is an example of a short-term goal. In just a few seconds, you analyse the situation, plan your shot, visualise the desired result and do your best to execute correctly.

You can also set short-term goals within a match. For example, in the first hour of play, you want to out-score your opponent.

Short-term goals can also be goals to achieve in a day, week, and month. Whether team or individual goals, it is important to constantly remind yourself (and your team) of what these goals are. Again, you do not need to physically record these on paper, but you do need to reaffirm them regularly.

Mid-Term Goals

Mid-term goals are those you wish to conquer in the upcoming 12 months. These should be updated quarterly and monitored one by one. A bowler should have no more than 10 mid-term goals at any one time.

Examples of mid-term goals for the upcoming twelve months could be things like winning the club championship singles, winning a regional event, improving long end draw shots or even being on time for every game in the year.

Long-Term Goals

Long-term goals are goals you set to achieve within the next five years. A bowler should have no more than three long-term goals. These goals are often the hardest to set as some may be achieved immediately while others may never even come close. Long-term goals give you a futuristic approach to what you want to achieve in bowls. The probability of achieving them may appear difficult at first but aiming high will lift the bar on your performance.

You should always draft your long-term goals before your mid-term goals. Once you have a clear guideline of what you want to achieve within five years, it is easier to set annual targets. Such annual targets should set the pathway for your long-term goals.

If long-term goals are not achieved within five years, you can re-set them again for the following five years.

Setting SMART Goals

Goal setting needs to be 'SMART'. The SMART model of Specific, Measurable, Achievable, Realistic and Timely gives you a framework for how to set proper goals.

<u>Specific Goals</u>
Specific goals are easily recognisable and deter you from setting general goals. A specific goal should answer questions such as Who, What, When and Why?

What do you want to achieve and why do you want to achieve it? Who is involved in this goal, and when do you want to achieve it?

For example, a specific goal could be identified as winning the club championship singles at your bowling club this season by focusing on your draw bowling.

Measurable Goals

Measurable goals ensure you can monitor and assess the progress of each specified goal. A measurable goal should answer questions such as how many and how much? Such goals need to be quantifiable, in other words, achievable or measurable in numbers.

For example, a measurable goal could be wanting your pennant team of 12 players to score 63 shots or more in a match over 63 ends, by using the team game plan.

Achievable Goals

Achievable goals are goals set that are not impossible. There is no point setting a goal in your first season of bowls to represent Australia within twelve months. You should always challenge yourself when setting goals but must make sure the goal is achievable. An achievable goal should answer questions such as, how?

For example, an achievable goal could be wanting to make the top-grade pennant side of your club within two years, by training harder than anybody else.

Realistic Goals

Realistic goals keep your goal setting on the straight and narrow. They are close-knit with achievable goals and ensure that what you target is realistic. Setting a mid-term goal to win the World Championship Singles would be an extremely unrealistic target.

As an example, a realistic goal could be scoring a personal best in the 48-bowl test in your next five attempts, by training minimum and maximum lengths at least once a week.

Timely Goals

Timely goals make sure you set an exact time or date for when you want to achieve the goal. The timeframe gives you a deadline, ensuring you work towards achieving the goal up until time expires. Setting goals with the ending time 'someday' or 'one day' are not timely. The goal is left open for too long, impossible to analyse and can encourage you to set it aside. You are more likely to stray from your avenue of achievement if your goal is not timely.

An example of a timely goal could be winning the club mixed pairs with your partner within the next two years, using a mixture of extremely long and short ends.

When you decide on a goal to achieve, read through this section again and make sure the target you set is SMART. If your goal lacks any of the five elements of SMART, it will fail to give you direction.

As an example, the end goal might be clear, but it might not explain how you plan to achieve the goal. If you set a goal to play in a higher grade, make sure you set a timely deadline and know specifically how you plan to achieve the goal.

Failure and assessment

When setting goals, you need to understand that failure is an option. A bowler who sets challenging SMART goals, will probably fail more than they achieve. From my own point of view, I have a high failure rate with mid-term and long-term. Even though my goals are SMART, they are extremely challenging because of the height of the bar I set. I am not afraid to fail, so long as I have something to aim for.

I discuss 'lessons of failure' in more detail later in the book but be aware that failure is part of sport. How you deal with that failure is what will separate you from the pack. All bowlers need to identify when they fail an attempted goal. The goal needs to be assessed and reset to a later date. It is important you understand why the attempt failed. You need to introduce ideas that combat the previous failure, increasing your probability of achieving the goal the next time around. By assessing a failed goal, you learn from the failure and expand your experience.

CHAPTER 20

Developing a Game Plan

A game plan is a preconceived strategy on how to win a match. As with setting goals, a game plan provides a clear understanding of how to achieve your desired result. In this case, the proposed target is to win.

Whether playing singles or a team event, you must have a game plan. Clearly knowing your game plan before starting a match will give you a greater probability of success.

Game Plan - Singles
A singles game plan must include all the following factors:
- Length to play
- Least favoured length to play
- Green speed and condition

- Opponent
- Your limits
- Mode of aggression
- Plan B + Trigger
- Plan C + Trigger

An example of a singles game plan in a 25-up contest could be as follows:
- Length to play: Ditch to ditch
- Least favoured length to play: Three quarter length
- Green speed: 11-12 seconds (Very Heavy)
- Green condition: Known to be unreliable with obvious tracks
- Opponent: High quality with no obvious weakness
- Your limits: Backhand weighted shots are inconsistent
- Mode of aggression: Attack on short ends, be defensive on long ends
- Plan B: If being outplayed, bring the mat right up the green and roll the jack to the two-metre mark to encourage aggression. Plan B triggers when 6 shots behind and in control of the mat
- Plan C: Resort to following the opponent's hand of play, sticking purely to the draw as an effort to gain some consistency. Plan C triggers when 10 shots behind, or when 6 shots behind and not in control of the mat

A basic game plan such as the example above will provide you with a clear direction of how to play a match of singles. If you fall behind in a game, you have clear trigger points of when to incorporate Plan B or Plan C. If you are less than six shots behind, then you stick to your original game plan. A seasoned singles player will have a stack of game plans, including certain plans for specific opponents and different plans for fast and slow greens.

You should regularly assess your game plan over time and adjust, as necessary. Successfully executing a regular game plan might make you predictable, but it can instil fear among your opposition. Even if they can predict exactly what you are going to do, they still need the skill to negate your qualities and execute their own game plan. Your game plan could take your opposition completely out of their comfort zone.

Game Plan - Team

When talking about a team game plan, we talk about your team of two, three or four, and your pennant side of 8, 12 or 16. In pennant, I believe it is advantageous to allow each skip to set their own team game plan. What one team may favour could be the downfall of another and vice versa.

When developing a team game plan for a fours match, you need to include similar factors to your singles game plan:
- Team length to play
- Least favoured team length of play
- Green speed and condition
- Opponents (all four)
- The limits of you and your team

- Mode of aggression
- Plan B + Trigger
- Plan C + Trigger

An example of a team game plan in a 21-end game of pennant could be as follows:

- Team length to play: As short as possible with the mat on the 2-metre mark
- Least favoured team length of play: Full-length ends
- Green speed: 15 seconds
- Green condition: Perfect
- Opponents (all four): Both the lead and second are known to be inconsistent. The third is a competitive player but is erratic with weighted shots. The skip loves to attack and is suspect when having to draw under pressure
- The limits of you and your team: Lead dislikes playing the narrow hand and second has no accurate weighted shot. Third can be nervous when drawing under pressure but has an accurate drive. Skip is a very solid draw bowler and prefers not to play weight to the head
- Mode of aggression: No aggression whatsoever from the lead or second. Both will play leading roles during the match, staying on the wide hand where possible. The third will be used to attack heads when down, or if a congested head needs to be broken, or to cover danger areas when the head lie is positive. Skip will play defensively when heads are not favourable and rely on the draw shot to save negative heads

- Plan B + Trigger: If opponent wins four or more ends in a row, the leader will change their hand regardless of how well they are bowling. The skip will take more risks calling the head for the second and third, including early attack and chasing the shot. If the tactic does not work, the skipper will rely on their drawing skills to save a vulnerable head position or large count
- Plan C + Trigger: Third to come to the head if we are seven or more shots down at any stage and have a 50/50 input on calling the shots with the skip. Third will then play what they see on the head without the skipper's involvement. This plan is extremely successful when the skipper is down on confidence, potentially calling negative heads. By giving the third authority to play the shot they favour, the skip is more likely to be up on the head than in previous ends. If the tactic fails, the skip must save the head position with skilful draw bowls. This plan continues until an end is won. The team will then have a mid-rink discussion, decide a change of length and the third will continue to stay at the same end as the skipper

It is essential to have a team game plan. If every player is aware of their role during a match, they are more likely to perform better. Each team member will be aspiring to win the match by following the same, clear guidelines. When behind in a match, the team are fully aware of the trigger points of Plan B and C, and what their new role will entail. A team will have a higher probability of coming back in a match if they stick together when behind on the scoreboard.

Once a game plan is proven to be successful, a team will develop the confidence that they can win any match, regardless of the score. The team will never accept defeat.

CHAPTER 21

Comfort Zone

Your comfort zone is one of the three psychological states of performance. In your comfort zone, you are at ease, feel familiar, believe you are in control, show low anxiety, and are generally consistent. For lack of a better term, your comfort zone is your 'happy place'.

Three Performance Zones

The three performance zones are:
- Comfort Zone
- Learning Zone
- Danger Zone

Imagine a circle where your comfort zone is the centre. The ring outside your comfort zone is the learning zone, while the outer ring is the danger zone. To achieve optimum performance levels on a regular basis, you need to expand your comfort zone, by regularly entering the learning zone.

The learning zone is where you focus on a level of competence outside of your comfort zone, or what you have already mastered. Entering the learning zone means a higher level of challenge, a potential increase in failure, and a broadening of your scope of achievement.

The danger zone is where you have not only left your comfort zone, but jumped over the learning zone. It is where you feel uneasy, are unfamiliar, lose control, have high anxiety and are totally inconsistent. You will enter the danger zone if you adopt too many new things into your game at the same time. Leaving your comfort zone must be well-balanced to ensure you will avoid this zone.

Why Leave Your Comfort Zone?

I was once a believer that my game plan, if mastered, could beat anyone, anytime, on any surface, in the world. I felt that by focusing on a simplified training regime, and becoming the best at certain skills, that I could win any title I set my mind on. This worked to a certain degree, but when challenged by an opponent at my own strengths, I had no alternatives to rely upon.

I became completely predictable and one-dimensional and was forced to find a way to expand my game.

Growing your game is a good reason to leave your comfort zone and enter the learning zone. You may be an excellent ditch-to-ditch draw bowler, but your short ends and weighted shots are below par. When challenged at your own length, and being beaten, you have no other option but to continue playing long ends. Some greens may be unplayable around the two-metre marks, or have downhill ditches, so playing full-length can end up a scrappy affair where neither player has an advantage. You may choose to incorporate more short-end play into your training program, so that later on you have this option in a match without increasing your anxiety or feeling out of control.

Leaving your comfort zone will provide a number of new challenges. You need to find the balance between training your strengths, your weaknesses, and also introducing new facets to your game, without increasing your training load. If you train too hard or too fast, you could create unwanted anxiety and end up in the danger zone. New challenges will increase your arousal, as learning a new skill or developing a new part of your game, will give you pleasure. If you don't challenge yourself, you will never leave the comfort zone.

When training new elements of your game, you must expect a rise in mistakes and failure. Sometimes you believe you have added new ammunition to your game, as you have been executing your new skill well in training. When brought to a match, you find the under-developed skills let you down, and you end up failing. Do not let failure deter you from introducing new ideas to your game, just treat it as a sign that you need to work a little bit longer on that area before trying it again in a match. Remember that you may have many years of training under your belt for comfort zone strengths. Any new skills may take months or years to develop before you can confidently use them in a match. As an idea, it took me almost a decade of short-end training before I could confidently roll a short jack in a game of singles.

Moving into the learning zone helps you confront your fears. Leaving your happy place may make you feel scared or uneasy, but by facing your fears, you can develop the courage to conquer them. Whether it takes mere weeks of training, or in my case almost a decade, overcoming a fear allows you to expand your comfort zone. Once your newly learnt skill proves successful in a match and you have the self-belief and confidence to use it, that new skill becomes part of your comfort zone.

By expanding your comfort zone, you are giving yourself more opportunities to achieve. If your preferred strengths are not working in a match, you have the option of confidently changing to an alternative strength. During a long event, it is unlikely that you can rely on one style of play without suffering defeat or elimination.

How to Leave Your Comfort Zone

It is one thing to know why you should leave your comfort zone, but another to learn how to do it. Finding the training balance to leave your comfort zone, will take some trial and error. Re-setting your whole program to new ideas will probably result in a drop in your preferred skills, confusion about what to train, and loss of control in match play. Going too hard too early, can see you end up in the danger zone. If you regularly visit the danger zone, you are more likely to skip back to your comfort zone and be unwilling to leave it.

Small steps are the key to leaving your comfort zone. Set goals to master one new skill or strength at a time. If the new skill becomes boring or tedious, feel free to mix up your challenges. Remember though, that you are unlikely to use a skill in a match until you have mastered the basics of the skill and conquered your fear. Although swapping your challenges may increase your interest in training, it is likely to take longer for the skill to actually form part of your game.

Learning to accept and appreciate change, is a good way to cope with leaving your comfort zone. Introduce the change with an open mind and recognise that although it may be tough at first, it will eventually be rewarding. Wanting to improve your game is hard. If it were that easy, then everyone would be doing it. You should appreciate the benefit of gaining a new skill or strength, and use that acquisition as your motivation.

Finally, be aware that your comfort zone is a personal space. What may work for you, may not work for others. When coaching, you must respect that your strengths may be someone else's weaknesses, and vice versa. Always appreciate that any changes you make to a bowler could pull them away from their happy place, so do so gently.

PART E

Personality

CHAPTER 22

Preparation

Preparation is setting goals, developing a game plan, and your thoughts and actions leading up to a match. Goal setting and game plan come under the umbrella of 'planning preparation', while thoughts and actions are 'personality preparation'.

Personality Preparation

Personality preparation is most effective when dealt with individually. There are times when you need a coach to help you prepare, or a team will have a group chat before a match, but the bulk of your personality preparation needs to be done alone. You need to make the choice to prepare the best way possible for you, even if your next match is a team game.

Bowlers who make an elite level such as State teams or National teams, are often forced to alter their preparation. Taking a bowler out of their comfort zone will generally result in a lower standard of performance. One of the biggest mistakes a coach can make, is dragging individual players away from what makes them comfortable.

A team is likely to perform better if every individual is playing better. The best way of achieving this is to grant the players the freedom to prepare individually. In an elite environment, bowlers are generally selected because of past performances and achievements. Changing the way these bowlers prepare, removes them from their comfort zone and puts them on a path to failure. A bowler can become disoriented or confused, completely uncomfortable and most likely fail at the first hurdle.

Bowls is an amateur sport, so club bowlers are likely to have more freedom to prepare for pennant however they choose. Aside from a training session once a week and the possibility of a team meeting immediately before a game, the individual is responsible for their own preparation. Bowlers who regularly play below standard in pennant, may need intervention by a coach. The coach can not only assist with delivery errors but discuss personality preparation with the individual.

Preparation is not to be confused with routine; they are distinctly different. The way you set-up to deliver a bowl is your routine, not preparation. Familiarise yourself with the terminology so you do not confuse one with the other.

Preparation Equals Performance

To prepare well for a match or event, you need to do all the things that make you feel comfortable. Superstitious people will need to undertake certain tasks leading into a match.

Everybody will prepare differently, and in some situations, preparation can be interrupted by external factors. Such factors could involve things like family or work. Although you should do all you can to prepare for a good performance, you must accept that some external factors are beyond your control. Instead of falling victim to the situation, use your knowledge as a creator. You must believe the change in preparation is a challenge. A challenge is merely a bump in the road on the way to your end goals, not a complete persecution. A change to your preparation might be irregular, but it is uncommon. Acknowledge the situation for what it is and do not allow it to distract you from your end goal.

The key to consistent, high-level performances, is to find the preparation that best works for you. If you are unsure what makes you play well, there is a simple task you can undertake to discover your optimum preparation.

For a month, record your daily activities and performances in diary. At the end of the month, you can highlight your best and worst performances. See if you can identify any trends in your preparation that led you to play well or to play poorly. This could include things like what you ate the night before, what you did in the morning leading up to the match, what time you arrived at bowls and even what grip you used.

I found this exercise to be extremely rewarding. I was able to identify trends in preparation that increased or decreased my level of performance. Sometimes it is impossible to prepare exactly aligned with the positive trends, but use of one or more of these trends generally results in an above par performance.

These positive trends include:
- Eating a high carbohydrate meal for dinner the night before play
- Arriving at a match no earlier than thirty minutes prior to the roll-up
- Sleeping in my own bed the night before
- Driving to a match myself and not getting a lift with team-mates
- At least two coffees prior to the game

When away on State representation, I am not able to sleep in my own bed and generally not able to drive myself to the match. I make a concerted effort to always include the other three points in my preparation.

Some of the negative trends I identified include:
- Not getting at least six hours sleep the night before
- Long travel on the day of play
- Not using my favourite bowls cloth

- Drinking too much alcohol the night before
- Rushing in the morning to get ready for play

Some of the negative trends are common sense, but may not necessarily have the same impact on your performance. It is important you undertake this activity yourself. Individuals may have similar trends to others, but identifying your own personal trends is critical to your level of performance.

Once you have found your ideal preparation, your chances of achieving a good performance are dramatically increased. You will know exactly what to encourage and avoid leading into a match. Eventually this preparation will go from process to habit. You should review this exercise every two to three years. As you get older, new trends might appear and should be included.

CHAPTER 23

Routine

A sound routine is absolutely critical in bowls. Your routine is your pre-shot set-up and delivery of the bowl. You need to rely on your routine, especially when under pressure. A flawless routine and delivery will enable you to achieve a higher percentage of shot success. In other words, it will help you achieve your set goals and desired results.

A routine needs to incorporate all of the following:
 - Pre-shot visualisation
 - Footwork and stance
 - Familiarisation of line and length
 - Focused eye point
 - Deliberate backswing
 - Flowing forward swing
 - Early analysis

Pre-shot Visualisation

Visualisation is the few seconds spent behind the mat, where you visualise the shot you are playing before you play it. I cover visualisation in more detail later in this section.

Footwork and Stance

You need to enter the mat with consistent and repetitive footwork. Moving millimetres on the mat will upset your visualisation and grass-line. This movement will impact on the likely success of the shot. If uncomfortable, you should leave the mat and start again.

You should always enter the mat with your non-stepping foot. This foot should point in the direction of your grass-line. The stepping foot will then follow and line up parallel with the non-stepping foot, pointing directly at your aiming point. Both feet should be at least a bowl's width distance apart and not close together. Once the stepping foot is pointing in the right direction, any movement to the non-stepping foot will not affect the line of a bowl, but can result in hips and shoulders facing the wrong direction. You should make an appointment with your club coach to discuss footwork and stance options.

Familiarisation of Line and Length

Once pre-shot visualisation and stance and footwork are complete, you need to concentrate your efforts on line and length. Although your stepping foot is already pointing at your aiming line, your eyes need to make contact. Your initial focus will be on your aiming point. You then glance at the jack for familiarisation of length. When comfortable, your head will move back to your aiming point.

Focused Eye Point

Once comfortable with your aiming point, you can draw your eye line back to a spot on the green approximately 2-4 metres in front of the mat. This spot becomes the new aiming point. You will stare at this point for the rest of your delivery action, right up until the bowl passes through the selected spot.

Deliberate Backswing

Your backswing needs to be deliberate and purposeful. The pendulum swing is useful for green speeds of 13-16 seconds but is limited on ultra-slow or ultra-fast greens. For this reason, I encourage a swing that changes speed depending on the green speed and the length of the end.

You will always have exactly the same starting point with your bowl, deliberately bringing the bowl back to the same point, and then allowing a flowing forward swing to the same point. Your delivery should be exactly the same; merely faster or slower depending on green speed and the length of the end.

Flowing Forward Swing

Your flowing forward swing will aim directly at your focused eye point and follow through until your hand reaches your eye line. A jolting or flicking style, will have an impact on your weight control.

Remembering the length of jack you have already familiarised with, you should follow through your focused eye point fluently. Your step will automatically adjust for the change of length, so there is no need to think about it at all.

Early Analysis

Early analysis is conducted on your line as you watch the bowl pass over your focused eye point. Once the bowl clears this spot, you can lift your head and begin analysing the weight of your bowl. It is important that you train 'running over' the focused eye point. A decent bowler should be able to hit the spot at least 17 times out of 20 and an elite bowler, at least 19 times out of 20. If you are not hitting the focused eye point regularly, then making a correction to grass-line is almost impossible.

How I Deliver a Bowl – My Routine

My routine takes approximately 15-20 seconds to complete. I have trained this to a level where it has become a robotic habit. Regardless of green speed or length of play, my delivery will always look the same; merely delivering the bowl in a faster or slower action as required.

My routine is as follows:

1. Stand behind the mat and visualise the shot I am about to play

2. Select a grass-line on the bank. Pay attention to whether the mat has moved from the two-metre mark and adjust accordingly (1 mat in for every 4 mats up)

3. Enter the mat with my non-stepping foot and bring forward my stepping foot

4. Turn my back foot inward to create the same balance as a shooter, and ensure my hips and shoulders are pointing at my aiming line

5. Focus on my line on the bank, then look at the jack for distance and return to my fixed aiming point

6. Bring my eye line down to the focus point and bowl over the spot, remembering the length of the end

7. Watch my bowl pass over or miss the spot

8. Analyse the weight of my bowl until it comes to rest, noting any quicker or slower parts on the green

9. Make mental note of any failure in line or weight and attempt to correct as necessary with my next bowl

Everyone will feel comfortable with their own tailored routine. Any of the above points can be changed to match what makes you feel comfortable.

Any new routine, or a modification to your current routine, will take up to 2,000 repetitions before it becomes a habit. If you have recently seen your club coach, then it is important to repeat any change of routine as many times as possible. The only way the changes can become natural, is if they become a habit and form part of your pre-delivery routine.

If your delivery is not flawless and comfortable, how do you expect to perform under pressure?

CHAPTER 24

Training

The term 'practice' does not sit well with me. Practice is when you jump on the green, put a jack up one end, play your four bowls, place a jack at the other end and repeat over and over again. Practice is beneficial when working on your delivery and routine, but outside that, has no real benefit to your game of bowls. Often, there is no thought to the length of play, or any real determination to work on a weakness.

If I had a dollar for every-time I watched a bowler 'practice' for two hours without moving the jack or changing the length, I could own my own small city. Seeing a bowler bring the mat up about 2-3 metres from the two metre-mark, and bowl continuous short to three-quarter ends, really puts a bee in my bonnet. The percentage of bowlers who choose to practice over train, is higher than you would believe.

I conducted a secret survey in 2015 over a two-week period. In that time, I watched 108 players come to the bowling club for a roll-up. Of those 108 players, only 12 chose to train; the other 96 were merely practicing. In percentage terms, 89% of bowlers who came for a roll-up chose to practice over train. I admit that my recordings only cover a small sample, but no matter where I go to roll-up, the trend is similar.

What is Training?

Training is where you plan your session on the green, work on specific attributes of your game, improve weaknesses and develop your overall game.

You need to set yourself a weekly training regime. Extra training for specific upcoming events can be added to this basic schedule. When done purposefully, training will escalate your overall game. No-one scores any shots or wins any games in training. Training is not a competition; it is a time to work on specifics, your own game plan, and the game plan of your team.

If you have a busy calendar of events, your training schedule may need to be altered from time-to-time. For the common club bowler, a training regime will generally remain uninterrupted, allowing you to repeat the process each week.

To help you get started, a basic regime such as the following may assist:

Weekly Training Program

<u>Monday:</u>
Rest day or day off

<u>Tuesday:</u>
45 minutes of dedicated training to areas of weakness, and facets of your game that faltered in your last match. After 45 minutes, take a 15-minute break and have a drink of water. Return to the green for a second session of 45 minutes, playing four short, four medium and four maximum length ends

<u>Wednesday:</u>
Reserved for specific events training for a maximum of one hour

<u>Thursday:</u>
45 minutes of dedicated training of your strengths. After 45 minutes, take a 15-minutebreak and have a drink of water. As Thursday is the most common pennant training night, you should devote 90 minutes to team training.

Your initial 45 minutes (and your short break) may need to be moved to make-way for team training. If you cannot arrive earlier than scheduled team training, complete your 45 minutes after the team session

<u>Friday:</u>
Rest day, day off or reserved for events training for a maximum of one hour

<u>Saturday:</u>
Pennant, tournament, or rest day

<u>Sunday:</u>
Reserved for championships, tournaments, or other events. If nothing is scheduled, use Sunday as a time to brush up on your mental toughness or have a rest day

The above regime requires a minimum of four hours of dedicated training per week and should be used as the minimum requirement. If you include training for specified events, you may train up to six hours per week. It is always a good idea to save some time to work on your mental toughness. As your physical game needs training, so does your mental game.

Take note that some sessions last for one and a half hours, with the session split in half. Once you reach 45 minutes of dedicated individual training, your body will begin to tire, and concentration will start to waiver. The 15-minute break in between, is to refresh, hydrate and relax, preparing you for the second half of the session. If you do not take a short break, the productiveness of your session will fall as the length of time increases. In most cases, you are better off training alone for just 45 minutes if you choose to disregard the break.

Training Attitude

How you train is an attitude choice. The mantra of your training should be to 'train as though you were playing a match'. Every bowl in your training should be delivered with purpose and importance. You should follow your routine for every delivery and make the most out of each bowl you play. If you are not weary or tired after a training session, it is a sign that you haven't fully committed. You should walk from the green with a feeling that your training achieved something, so reward yourself with a cold drink and some time to sit down and relax.

<u>Training Alone</u>
When training specific areas of your game, it is important you train alone. Another visitor to your rink may distract you from your training plan and halve the amount of bowls you play in the session. It may also start idle chit-chat, which not only influences your session goals, but affects your concentration and focus.

You should have at least three 45-minute training blocks per week, where you are the only person on the rink.

<u>Training for an Event</u>
Wednesday and Friday are generally the best days to train for an upcoming event. You may be in an event such as the Club Sin-

gles that weekend, or playing a new position in a tournament or in pennant.

Event training sessions should go no longer than one hour. A solid 45 to 60-minute session on event specifics, is more than sufficient.

Short and Sharp

As you have learnt, it is inefficient to train for periods longer than 45 minutes alone, or 90 minutes in a team, without having sufficient breaks in between. Every individual is different, but your body will always reach a point of lethargy that makes continuous training useless. Any further training at this time, will see a lapse in concentration, physical delivery mistakes and more than likely, will teach you next-to-nothing.

Remember that short and sharp training sessions will be far more beneficial than hours of bowling on end. Training should be a purposeful and enjoyable exercise of self-improvement, not a show-off, three-hour practice session, of getting bowls close to the jack on your favourite length of play.

Training should be planned and specific. It should be done in short and sharp bursts covering areas of weakness, strength, and team training. A solid training regime will help you improve your game, achieve better results, and reach set goals.

A Final Thought on Training

You have learnt that training is more beneficial than practice. If my sample survey indicates that 89% of bowlers choose to practice instead of train, does that mean 89% of bowlers are stupid? Does that mean only 11% of bowlers choose to purposefully work on their game? Maybe it does.

Next time you go for a roll-up, make sure you follow your weekly training regime.

If you plan to practice instead of train, stay home and weed your garden; at least that way you will do something productive with your time.

CHAPTER 25

Visualisation of Shot-Play

Visualisation is the mental image you create prior to entering the mat to bowl. It is a process of acknowledging the shot to be played, viewing the grass-line and weight of a bowl, and identifying the desired result.

Visualisation is regarded as paramount at the elite level. A bowler who visualises the shot prior to execution, will claim that their success rate is higher. If 'like attracts like', then thinking about a shot and visualising a positive outcome, will generally attract a positive result. It is not a guaranteed method of success, but it will improve your chances.

To visualise a shot, you need to create a mental image. You must block out all external senses. The slightest smell, sound, or visual interference may distract your visualisation. If you lose attention, you need take a breath and start again. When initially introducing visualisation to your delivery routine, you are likely to be distracted regularly.

If you train purposefully and with intent, you can build your visualisation skills. One of the main reasons I suggest that you train as though you are playing a match, is to ensure that each bowl you deliver in training, goes through your normal delivery routine. As well as solidifying your action, you are developing your visualisation skills.

Many people find visualisation easier when they close their eyes. As like in a dream, you can see mental imagery clearer, with the external senses shut down. This is not a practical method in bowls. You need to be able to visualise with your eyes open. By standing behind the mat and creating a mental image of your grass-line and finishing point or result, you have essentially planned for the event that is about to occur. You have successfully applied visualisation.

Do not be concerned if you are struggling to apply visualisation to your routine. It is not uncommon for many bowlers to try it out and shortly after, give up, claiming that it is too difficult. It may take years to master, but certainly worth considering if you want to improve your game.

If the best bowlers in the world claim that pre-shot visualisation is critical to their routine, then it is probably worth paying attention. If you believe the visualisation to be true, then you will likely attract the desired result.

CHAPTER 26

Superstition

Superstition is defined as the widely held, but irrational belief in supernatural influences, especially leading to good luck or bad luck, and the practice of that belief.

Obsessive Compulsive Disorder (OCD) is often compared to superstition, as both are considered coping strategies. There are three main differences between superstition and OCD:
1) Superstition is where you feel you need to do something to cope, while OCD means you must do something to cope
2) Unlike Superstition, OCD controls all aspects of your daily life
3) Superstition is a choice. OCD is not a choice, it is a mental illness

Is Superstition Healthy?

Most superstitions are fun and harmless.

As a child, your parents probably told you that coming across a black cat, opening an umbrella inside, or walking under a ladder were all bad luck. Smashing a mirror would lead to seven years of bad luck, while anything to do with the number 13 would be a disaster.

You were probably also told that a rabbit's foot, knocking on wood, and a four-leaf clover were all signs of good luck. These age-old superstitions have been passed through generations for hundreds of years.

In our sport, most bowlers have at least one superstition. Some of the common bowling superstitions that I have come across include:
- Using the same bowls cloth
- Stepping onto the rink first
- Winning the toss
- Not wearing bowls shoes while travelling to a game
- Eating the same breakfast or lunch

Most bowling superstitions are completely harmless. They generally arise when you couple a memorable match with non-relevant factors. Unconsciously, you have applied classical conditioning. If done regularly, superstition can become a habit and inadvertently form part of your preparation.

Superstition and Preparation

Whether you are superstitious or not, you must understand that it is an irrational belief to think superstition will bring you good luck. If your preparation involves superstition, you may have a longer or more detailed preparation than others. This is okay, so long as you can devote the time you need, to feel in control.

In reality, whether you act on your needs or not, superstition will have no bearing on the result. If it helps you start a match feeling comfortable, then by all means continue to be superstitious. Just be weary that your superstitions can change from time to time depending on your results, and that your preparation may need to change also.

Superstition is a Choice

You decide whether to be superstitious or not. As most of the superstitions in bowls are harmless, whether you are superstitious or not doesn't matter. Superstition only becomes an issue when you are unable to act on your feelings, and believe that inability will cause you to lose.

As superstition only makes you 'feel' you need to do something to cope, the way you react to the thought is up to you. You have learnt that feelings are only thoughts and that you do not need to accept them as your choice of action. You might have conditioned yourself to a point where your feelings need to be acted upon, but this can always be reversed. If superstition is controlling your game, then I suggest you look at re-conditioning yourself. Any negative distraction in a match will only attract negative ramifications to your overall performance.

I used to be superstitious, but over time I grew out of it. I found it to be a time-consuming experience that provided no benefit to my overall game.

PART F

Stress

CHAPTER 27

Anxiety

Anxiety is an intense feeling of worry, nervousness, or unease about something with an uncertain outcome. Anxiety is a form of severe stress, where your mind and body cannot distinguish between what is real and what is merely a thought. It can lead to moments of total and utter confusion as well as other side effects.

Anxiety confusion is extremely stressful and can result in:
- Excessive hot or cold sweats
- Increased heartrate
- Clammy hands
- Feelings of unease
- Dizziness and fainting
- Nausea and vomiting
- The need to run away or escape
- Insomnia

- Body twitching or shakes
- Numbness

In its most serious form, anxiety can completely incapacitate a person from going about their normal day-to-day duties. Anyone who suffers regular bursts of anxiety should see a doctor immediately. As someone who has experienced frequent anxiety for almost two decades, I can't encourage you enough to seek professional help if anxiety is a problem for you. Early intervention could limit the severity of any potential mental illness.

Anxiety or Nerves?

In any game of bowls, there is a chance you will feel 'nervous' at one point or another. Before a game you may feel uneasy, worried about playing well or how the result of the game will pan out. During the game, you may be nervous about playing a shot, holding your breath while an opponent plays a bowl or even stressing over a head when you are down a large count. Even after a game, you may be worried about the backlash of playing poorly, or that you were integral to the loss.

You need to understand the difference between anxiety and 'nerves'. Nervousness is defined as being easily agitated or alarmed, or the inability to brace yourself mentally in a demanding situation.

Nerves are a natural response by your body to a stressful moment or event. Being nervous can bring about some symptoms of anxiety such as accelerated heartrate or clammy hands.

Anxiety is a disorder developed from a mixture of genetics, life events and brain chemistry. Unlike nerves, anxiety is long-lasting and can be triggered at any time, for no apparent reason.

What you are most likely to experience in bowls, is nervousness. Although anxiety can be treated, it cannot be cured. Nerves can be attached to a particular scenario or moment and can therefore, be overcome.

Overcoming Nerves

Dealing with nerves in a fast and efficient manner is important. The longer you feel nervous, the more likely you will become a victim of the nervousness. You need to apply stress-management as soon as nerves arise.

<u>Nerves in the Short-Term</u>
A good way to shake off nerves in the short-term, is to follow my motto of WERB; walk, eat, release, and breathe. Every individual will react differently to short-term stress management techniques, so choose the one or two that work for you and apply them to your game.

Walking: Walking off nerves is a quick and effective way of freeing your body from tension. A walk to the bathroom or a swift walk to the other end of the bowls head may be all you need to shake off the nerves

Eating: I find that eating, snacking, or drinking a cup of coffee mid-match can reduce nervousness. Carbohydrates increase the supply of serotonin to the brain. Serotonin is well known for its calming effect and is often referred to as the 'calming chemical'. Snacks such as lollies, crackers and bread are perfect examples of foods that can be eaten during a game. A high carbohydrate breakfast will ensure that you start a game relaxed. Try to avoid protein-based foods and fatty foods, as these thwart the production of serotonin. Eating fish, fries, potato chips or fast food, will prevent natural serotonin production and release, and leave you more susceptible to nervousness

Release: Many fiery characters benefit from an immediate release of tension. Stress and nerves can create 'nervous energy' and the release of this energy may be the best way to deal with the tension. If you ever see a bowler scream or yell, stomp their foot, or hit their leg, you can attribute that to a release of nervous energy. A more appropriate method of releasing tension is done using your two hands. Take a deep breath and hold it for 3-5 seconds. While holding your breath, use the thumb and index finger of one hand and push them together forcefully, until you feel the tension (3-5 seconds again). Slowly exhale and as you do, gradually release the tension between the finger and thumb. Repeat a couple of times and you should feel more relaxed than you were just moments earlier

Breathe: The final method I apply to reduce nervousness, is to take slow and deliberate breaths. This method is further beneficial when closing your eyes. By focusing on the breathing, you distract your mind from the stressful situation and inevitably relax the muscles throughout your body. In a psychological sense, this is an extremely basic introduction to 'mindfulness'. A deep breath before every bowl will help relax the body prior to delivery. Two minutes of deep breathing while awaiting your turn can also be beneficial

Nerves in the Long-Term

Sorting out nervousness in the short-term has its benefits but ultimately, you should work on overcoming nerves for good. Being nervous from time to time is natural, but feeling nervous constantly, is a problem. You cannot expect to perform at your best, or for your delivery to hold up under pressure, if you let nerves take control of your mindset.

There are certain methods you can apply to assist with eradication of nervousness. If you believe nerves are affecting your performance, then consider introducing one or more of the following treatments:

Courage: Highlighted as one of the critical theories of mental toughness, courage allows you to beat nerves by willingly confronting your fears. If nerves come from agitation or being alarmed and are an inability to deal with a situation mentally, then they can be overcome with courage. You can confront your nerves by reminding yourself that nervousness is a natural human reaction. Acknowledge the nerves for what they are and politely dismiss them. Make the choice to be courageous and don't let nerves control your performance

Preparation: Planning and preparing for an event will settle your nerves far more than being unprepared. You should ratify or edit your game and then direct your focus to personality preparation. If you have completed your scheduled training, can achieve the right level of sleep, eat the right food, and complete as many positive preparation trends as possible, then you are likely to start a game relaxed. If nerves creep in during the match at any stage, and you have had a satisfactory preparation, then you can disregard them. All you can do is your best

Positivity: Having the ability to think positively and eliminate any negative thoughts, will likely impact on your level of nervousness. A positive thinker is a creator, who will recognise nerves as a challenge. When nerves become a factor, you must exercise the role of a coach and make the attitude choice to stay positive. Employ the empowerment dynamic and use it to disregard any nerves that can negatively affect your performance

Talk: If you are nervous, talk to someone. Sharing the burden of your nerves can halve their impact. In a team game, have a short discussion with your team-mates, or if skipping, start a conversation with the other skip. Cracking a joke or saying something humorous can instantly relax you. In singles, ask the marker a question or walk down to the head and have a brief chat with the marker there. A burden shared is a burden halved. You are not seeking a rescuer, merely relaxing yourself through chit-chat

Relaxation: Outside of bowls, there are many relaxation therapies available such as yoga, meditation, tai chi and hypnotism. If nerves have become a regular occurrence when bowling, you may benefit from an external relaxation therapy

Every individual has ideas on what works best for them. If you are struggling with nervousness, try one of the above techniques. If one doesn't work, try another one. Never let nervousness ruin your performance. Not only will you lose regularly, you will fail under pressure, and your overall enjoyment for bowls will suffer.

CHAPTER 28

Adrenaline

When the brain identifies an emotional stress or encounter, your body will automatically increase the production of adrenaline and cortisol.

Adrenaline speeds up your heart rate, raises your blood pressure and positively influences your energy levels.

Cortisol prepares your body for battle and sends you into damage repair.

Often when a match is tight or a key moment has occurred, your body will increase the production of adrenaline. Automatically, your heart rate will increase, and your blood pressure will rise.

Adrenaline is seen as a great benefit to athletes, as they appear to 'grow another leg'. In reality, adrenaline is dangerous and can encourage long-term health problems. A burst of adrenaline from time to time is considered natural, with the body returning to normal function after a few seconds. Concern arises when you repeatedly experience bursts of adrenaline. Over-exposure to adrenaline is known to increase your chances of depression, inconsistent sleep patterns, digestion problems and even obesity.

Take a step back for a second and realise that adrenaline is used on a patient when they are in cardiac arrest. Adrenaline is used to re-start a heart that has stopped beating. It is an immensely powerful drug, and in large doses, extremely dangerous.

When bowling, you may experience bursts of adrenaline from time to time. If you or your team-mate plays an amazing shot, you are likely to experience adrenaline. Naturally, the adrenaline should subside after a few seconds of thrill and no damage is done.

If your adrenaline fails to dissipate, or you are unable to control your flow of adrenaline, you are likely to make rash decisions, and be unable to stay relaxed on the mat. Adrenaline can send you into supreme confidence, so you must take the time to analyse each decision you make. Do not risk a drop in confidence because an over-exuberant plan goes wrong.

Drinking alcohol gives rise to adrenaline within your body. In small doses, alcohol is absorbed and processed by your body with little fuss or harm. In large doses, you can become intoxicated, losing your balance, co-ordination, and common sense. When you are tipsy or intoxicated, your decision making is severely impacted. If you compare excess adrenaline to intoxication, you end up with a similar result. Both are fine in moderation, but hazardous in high doses.

It is one thing to know what adrenaline is, but another to understand how to slow it down, and to return your body to normal functionality. Adrenaline is best when it is out of your system.

When you experience a burst of adrenaline, identify it, acknowledge it for what it is and supervise it. If the adrenaline has not disappeared within 30 seconds, you need to consciously push it away. Some ways you can clear your body of adrenaline is to:
- Take ten slow and deliberate breaths
- Close your eyes and hold your breath for 10 seconds, breathe 3 times, and then repeat
- Take a bathroom break for a minute or two to remove yourself from the situation
- Distract yourself from the situation by starting a conversation

If your adrenaline is not brought under control, your heart rate will continue to beat at unusually high levels. If your heart rate is higher than normal, it will be extremely difficult to stick to your normal routine. The natural reaction is to rush into a shot or to ignore one of the steps in your normal routine. This will not only affect the likelihood of shot success but leave you mentally volatile to a miss.

Even if you are successful with the shot, your adrenaline and heart rate may go even higher, which must prompt immediate action to consciously lower your adrenaline. If you play a poor bowl, your behaviour is likely to be volatile, which could also adversely affect your heart rate and adrenaline. Either way, adrenaline is best gone before you enter the mat to play your next bowl.

Bowlers play at their ultimate level when their heart rate is steady and normal. As soon as your heart rate rises above your average rate, you limit your chances of being successful. Adrenaline may make you feel great at the time, but like all good things, it is best consumed in moderation.

CHAPTER 29

Anger Management

Since the release of *In the Zone* first edition, there has been a rise in anger management research in sport. These studies have highlighted strategies that are known to suppress anger during a match.

Even in lawn bowls, people 'get angry' or 'lose their cool'. Bowlers often direct their anger at officials, spectators, equipment, and their opposition. Other bowlers struggle to suppress their anger as it arises, allowing it to build up internally. Eventually the bubble bursts, resulting in an unsightly external outburst.

A key development in my own game was learning to manage my anger. In the past, a bad situation or outcome would result in regular poor body language, a demonstration of anger, and a surrender to the drama triangle. As a victim of the anger, I would allow it to persecute me, snowballing until I lost the plot and exploded.

Managing your anger in lawn bowls is extremely important. If you want to achieve your goals, desired results and increase your chances of winning a match, you must suppress anger immediately. Short and sharp outbursts are not the answer. They might release internal anger, but they do not fix your anger issues.

Suppressing Anger in the Long-Term

Unsurprisingly, the solutions to controlling your anger relate to other discussions in this book. To suppress anger in the long-term, you can apply any of the following coping strategies:

<u>Mindful Breathing</u>
Deep mindful breathing will help distract you from any internal anger. Long and deliberate breaths will slow down your heart rate and relax your body. Focus on your breathing and ignore any external factors. Three deep breaths will only take 10-20 seconds and is known to suppress anger immediately. Completing these breathing exercises off the green is just as important as in a match. The more you train your breathing, the more likely it is to become habit.

Condition Yourself to Suppress Anger

Training anger management responses off the green will help you deal with anger in the heat of the moment. Your memory will trigger a response based on what you have conditioned and not necessarily on the anger. You can use classical conditioning and pair a song with your anger. Anytime you play the song in your head, it will have an instant calming effect. You can instrumentally reward yourself for anger suppression, while penalising yourself for outbursts of anger. Observing the grace and skill of a mentor and how they suppress their anger could also be beneficial.

Positive Thinking

Make the attitude choice to supress anger by encouraging positive thinking. One of the simplest things you can do when angry is to smile. You have already learnt the benefits of smiling, all which relax the body and promote positivity. The influx of positive thoughts can reduce or extinguish your anger and help revive your concentration to the task at hand.

Relaxation Methods

As discussed in the section on anxiety, relaxation methods are also beneficial to anger management. Yoga, meditation, tai chi and hypnotism are all accepted methods of relaxation. Adopting one of these methods as a hobby outside of bowls, could help get your anger under control.

Seek Professional Help

Anger isn't a disorder but can be a symptom of an underlying mental health issue. Excessive and regular outbursts of anger could be a sign of depression, bipolar disorder, obsessive compulsive disorder, abuse, or trauma, just to name a few. I am not a professional, nor attempting to diagnose your anger. I suggest that you seek professional help if you believe anger is not only influencing your game of bowls, but your day-to-day life.

You don't need to 'get angry' to 'get competitive'. In bowls, anger is not intimidating to a seasoned player. If anything, it is a sign of weakness that makes you come across as flustered, distracted and down on confidence. Any good bowler will see this as a time to put their foot down and take complete control of a match.

Anger in Young Bowlers

Young bowlers are especially vulnerable to anger. Having an immature and inexperienced mind, a younger person is more likely to express anger if they are confused, frustrated, scared or not in control. An under-developed mind has limited responses to negative situations, and displaying anger is a common response. A young bowler does not express anger because they are 'spoilt', 'entitled' or a 'little shit'. It is a natural, immature response, to a confronting situation.

If you are subject to anger by a younger bowler, the worst thing you can do is try to parent them. Remember back to what you learnt about conversation; any response to a child ego, must be done with an adult ego. Rather than responding with anger (child to child), telling them to grow-up (parent to child), or attempting to nurture them (parent to child), you should analyse the situation and attempt to control it (adult to child). Instead of giving advice or empathy during a match, you can use an ulterior transaction such as, "Your mother is watching", or attempt to calm them down by saying, "Don't let a game get the better of you".

Post-match, you can apply the parent ego. To gain their attention, show empathy and nurture them. If you gain their attention, your advice is more likely to be taken onboard. Most child egos will respect the advice of a parent ego once their emotions have calmed down. Relate to their anger with an example of your own and how you learnt to overcome your anger. If this particular young bowler is striving to reach higher levels in the future, such as State representation, you need to tell them that such behaviour will influence their selection. This awakening will hopefully help them to understand that anger is not a solution to any situation. It may not end the young bowler's anger, but at least they will think twice about it next time.

PART G

Success & Failure

CHAPTER 30

Lessons of Failure

Failure is defined as a lack of success in a set goal or objective. Failure is the self-perceived outcome of a situation where you miss a shot, lose a game, or are eliminated from an event.

A lot of bowlers marry failure with a negative result, but as failure is self-perceived, it can be attached to any situation you choose it to be. What you may treat as a failure, others may believe is a success and vice versa. As an example, you might collect a silver medal in a major event. You can believe the silver is a failure as you 'lost the gold', while others see 'winning the silver' as a success.

It is human nature to feel disappointed with failure. How you choose to react to the failure is what is most important. If you believe you have failed, then you have failed; regardless of what others believe. The only opinion on failure that truly matters is your own.

You can become a victim of failure. Instead of viewing failure as a challenge, or a bump in the road on the way to your long-term goals, you treat failure as a persecutor. Rather than instigating the empowerment dynamic and coaching your way past disappointment, you seek sympathy through a rescuer.

Overcoming Failure

I have developed 12 steps on how to deal with failure. To better deal with failure, you need to be familiar with all 12, and how each step will help you overcome even the most disappointing failures.

1) <u>Failure is an option</u>
If you want to achieve in bowls, you must accept that failure is an option. With every action, there is a positive or negative reaction. If you actively strive to win, you must accept that sometimes you are going to lose. If you set challenging goals, it is an unrealistic expectation to achieve every goal. If you are achieving every goal, then you are likely setting the bar too low in the first place.

2) Acknowledge a failure

When you fail, acknowledge that you have failed. When you accept that you have failed, you are able to trigger methods on how to best deal with a similar situation next time. Don't dwell endlessly on a failure, just accept the result and decide how you will move forward.

3) Appreciate how you feel about failure

It is human nature to feel awful, disappointed, and even disgusted with failure. Part of the healing process is to appreciate the way failure makes you feel. Failure does not decide how you react, but it does decide how you feel. Remembering how failure makes you feel is motivation to avoid it as much as possible in the future.

4) Accept appropriate responsibility

If you are unable to accept responsibility, or part of the responsibility of a failure, then you are less likely to do something about it. Once a failure has been acknowledged and you have absorbed the feelings, you must accept some sort of responsibility. Identifying what you were responsible for, can help you correct or work on those errors.

5) Learn from the failure

If you have acknowledged a failure, allowed it to sink in, and accepted responsibility, you can now begin to learn from the failure. You should treat failure as a way of identifying areas of your game that need improvement and further development.

Sometimes you do everything right leading into a match, play brilliantly, but still fail at the final hurdle. Review your performance and identify any areas you could have done better. You may have played at a high standard, but stumbled with nerves, negative thinking, or even over-confidence. No performance is ever perfect, so constantly attempt to perfect the areas that need the most attention.

6) Trending failure

If failure has become a regularity, you may need to review your preparation, goals, bowls delivery and style of play. The definition of an idiot is someone who chooses to do the same thing over and over again, expecting a different result. If you constantly experience failure, start with an appointment with your club coach. Make sure the fundamentals of your delivery are correct. Even bowlers at an elite level need regular supervision by a coach, as bad habits can creep in without knowing. Once your fundamentals are sorted, review your preparation and goals, and adjust them as necessary. Give yourself some time to reverse the failure trend and re-assess your position in a month.

7) Talk about failure

In the long run, talking about failure can be beneficial to your game. I am not referring to mid-match burden-sharing of your thoughts, but off the green discussions with a coach, mentor, friends, or family. Talking about failure can give you ideas of how to overcome it in the future. You talk about failure not to dwell on it, but to help expand your ideas on how to best deal with it and correct it. Do not use the talk as a sympathy hunt for a rescuer, raise your concerns and ask for the ideas and opinions of others. This brainstorm can help you make personal decisions on your best way forward.

8) <u>Be realistic with your thoughts</u>

Staying real with failure is extremely important. At times, failure may lead you to believe that you are a hopeless cause. Some failures can hurt so much, that being realistic with your thoughts can seem impossible. Remind yourself that failure is a sign of challenging yourself to do something difficult, that you can handle the failure, and that you can learn from the failure. Hopelessly procrastinating about the result is unhealthy and futile. You should direct your energy and thoughts on developing ways to reduce the probability of failing next time.

9) <u>Doing your best is not a failure</u>

If you have trained efficiently, prepared perfectly, and given your best in a game, you have not failed. You may feel that you have failed, but you must react positively. There may be an underlying reason for failure that has nothing to do with your performance. Sometimes your opponent is just 'too good' on the day. Punishing yourself for doing your best will cripple your positivity and self-belief. If necessary, direct your attention to your training and lead-up. One failure does not decide a career, so don't jump to conclusions about a single failure if it is an abnormal result in an otherwise successful trend.

10) Review your goals

Many bowlers experience regular failure because their goals are not SMART. Re-read the chapter on SMART goals and ensure your goals fit the criteria discussed. If you can record specific, measurable, achievable, realistic, and timely goals, then you will be clearer with what you want to achieve, and how you want to achieve it.

11) Face your fear of failure

The fear of failure is a common trend among bowlers, especially those at the elite level. It is human nature to worry about our seven basic needs, including esteem needs and self-actualisation. Those who fear they have 'more to lose' will often take failure more to heart. A bowler who makes a willpower choice to be courageous, should never fear failure. In a close game or an important moment, stare failure in the face, confront it, and dismiss it completely. If you ultimately become victorious, you will have defeated the fear of failure. Even if you lose, you can still acknowledge that you were not scared of failing. Fearing the end result before it happens will distract you from what is important in the present. Focus on the process.

12) Brush failure aside

Once the first 11 steps have been applied, you can finally brush aside the failure, no sooner, no later. Do not brush aside any failure immediately without first considering the lessons of failure. You may appear as though the failure has had little or no impact on you, but deep down, you know you have unfinished business. You will never learn from a failure if you sweep it under the carpet before you have assessed it properly. On the other hand, allowing yourself to dwell on a failure longer than necessary, can have long-term negative influences on your self-belief and positivity. Complete the analysis, learn from the failure and brush it off, like water off a duck's back. Forgive yourself and move on.

Over the course of my career, I have found failure to be the hardest hurdle to overcome. I often fall to levels so low, that I cannot escape the doldrums of defeat. Failure can absorb me and overwhelm all the positivity of my game. Whether mental illness contributes to my state of mind or not, I am determined to work on ways of better dealing with failure. I still struggle to overcome failure at times and continue to develop my attitude about mistakes and defeat. For me, it is constantly a work in progress, because I refuse to allow failure to consume me.

CHAPTER 31

Managing Success

Success is defined as the accomplishment of a goal or purpose. Success is addictive and many bowlers cannot enjoy our sport without regularly feeding their hunger to achieve.

Luckily in bowls, there are an enormous number of events to enter. From social club bowls and local tournaments, to club championships, zone and regional titles, State titles, and National titles, there is no reason why you cannot be successful from time to time.

Your level of success depends on the height of your goals. If you are a new bowler, or a bowler who has passed their prime, you may have goals to win social events and local tournaments. You may not even enter club championships or state events. On the other hand, an elite player might have goals of State titles and

National titles. They will probably not enter any social events or small club tournaments.

One thing is for certain, even though we can all be successful at one point or another, maintaining that success is a whole new kettle of fish.

Maintaining Success

I have developed 10 strategies on how to maintain success. To a degree, anyone in bowls can be successful once or twice, but maintaining that success over a long period of time separates a good bowler from a champion bowler. Instead of being 'a flash in the pan', there are methods designed to not only help you succeed, but to increase your likelihood of maintaining that success.

1) <u>Plan for success</u>
Set goals to plan for success. If you win a title or event without planning for it, you are likely to have rare or inconsistent success. Part of planning for success, is to give yourself clear guidelines and processes on how to achieve that success. You can adjust your training to prepare for a certain event, work on areas of your game that need development, or even devote more time to mental toughness. If you work more efficiently and effectively on designated plans, you should not be surprised if you are victorious.

2) Self-control

To maintain success, you need to prioritise what is important to you. Being able to say "no" can keep your priorities on track. If you are completing a 45-minute block of individual training, you need to disallow others on your rink. Further, being able to knock back offers of social bowling events in favour of rest, may be a wise decision. Do not overload yourself with bowls seven days a week, as you can lose interest and become stale. Use your self-control to achieve a career balance.

3) Stay humble

Despite your level of success, you should always be respectful and humble. No-one likes a bad loser, but no-one likes an arrogant winner either. In my mind, the difference between being a winner and a champion, is that a champion is always respectful and humble. In important finals, always take the time to acknowledge your opposition and their efforts, be thankful to your support crew and the officials, and always recognise the contribution of sponsors. You should also accept congratulatory messages sincerely and thank anyone who congratulates you.

4) Be realistic

There will be times across your career when you are winning regularly, and other times when you can't seem to win a thing. Be realistic about your trend of performances and if required, make small adjustments to your training, preparation, and game plan. If you had previously enjoyed a run of success and now find yourself missing out on the big wins, drastic changes to your game will only compound the failures and take you too far out of your comfort zone. You may be closer to a win than you think.

5) Positivity

It is no surprise that positivity can help you maintain success. You might find it easier to be positive if you are regularly winning, but must also stay positive when results trend against you. In fact, being positive about your game when things are tough, will shorten the period to your next success. Being positive may seem like common sense, but human nature decides that you feel down and disappointed during periods of failure. If you choose to react positively and work on areas that need improvement or alteration, your path back to success takes a decent short-cut.

6) Ride the wave of success

When winning an event, you should always take the time to celebrate your victory. Depending on the magnitude of your title, you should celebrate accordingly. A club championship singles might mean a few drinks after the game, while a State singles might mean a dinner out with family and friends, or a night away with your partner. You should plan your method of success shortly after victory, ensuring the celebrations do not distract you from your next event.

7) The law of attraction

If 'like attracts like', then success attracts more success. This is true, but regular success also attracts others who have regular success. The pointy end of a big event will often see similar names making an appearance. To win these events, you need to be able to defeat other bowlers who are also regular achievers. At this stage, your game plan becomes the most crucial item of interest. Depending on your opponent, you can make small adjustments to your game plan, keeping your strengths at the forefront, while negating the strengths of your opposition. When playing in a match that is likely to be close, the bowler who enforces the most superior plans and tactics, will likely win.

8) Forgive yourself

If you are eliminated in an event, it is important to follow the lessons of failure. Once you reach the final step and brush the failure aside, you must forgive yourself for the failure. Forgiveness allows you to put the past behind you and move on. Set your attention to the next event and begin planning on how to win that.

9) Emotional intelligence

Through success, you must have the intelligence to constantly keep your emotions in check. Having the skill to identify negative thoughts, acknowledge them for what they are, and replacing with a positive thought, is a good example of emotional intelligence. Should your emotions ever overwhelm your positivity and self-belief, you are more likely to fail. How you feel is not what is important, it is how you choose to act or react that is.

10) <u>Review goals regularly</u>

As you become more successful, you need to review your goals on a regular basis. Setting the bar higher each time will give you new motivation and direction for success. Winning the club championship singles might be a goal of yours, but it should never end there. On victory, you should re-set the goal to win your region or zone. A club championship is only the starting point to a Regional, State, National and World title. Keep moving the bar higher each time you achieve a goal. With a clear direction on what to aim for, you are more likely to achieve regular success.

CHAPTER 32

Winning, Losing & Review

Learning how to be a gracious winner and a respectful loser is all part of playing sport. Not only this, understanding how to take a win or loss internally, is critical to staying in a positive frame of mind.

There are two golden rules to the outcome of any match:
1) If you win, enjoy your victory, plan your celebration, and move on to your next game; and
2) If you lose, learn from the experience, review your performance, brush it away, and move on to your next event.

Winning

As a gracious winner you must always be respectful to your opponent, even if the score line is embarrassing for them. Taking the time to offer an opponent a cold drink or answering some of their questions about the match is always a good start. Even if you need to rush off to your next game, your opponent may have questions to ask. Always spare a moment to give them any advice or assistance they request. Even in defeat, an opponent will have far more respect for you, if you grant them the time afterwards.

You should enjoy every victory you have, even if you were expected to win. By celebrating the result, you are moulding yourself into a winner. The enjoyment and celebration will make you want to win regularly. Mentally, you want to win so that you can enjoy the winning feeling. You should feel proud and satisfied that your game plan was successful. Train your body to enjoy winning.

Losing

As a respectful loser, despite how awful you feel inside, you will always shake the hand of your opponent, look them in the eye, and congratulate them. Even if you have just played the worst game of your life, you need to be respectful enough to state 'well-played' or 'too good'. The game is over and nothing you can do from that point can change the outcome of the match.

A loss will make you upset and disappointed with the outcome. Emotion aside, a loss should start an instant chain of events for you, and this does not begin with a dozen heavy drinks at the bar. A loss or failure should trigger the 12 lessons of failure.

The outcome of a match, especially when the game is tight, will cause powerful and emotional thoughts. That split-second reaction will define your character as a bowler. Make sure you think before you act.

Review

The key reasons behind reviewing each of your performances, whether you have won or lost, is to determine:
    a) What you could have done better
    b) What you learnt from the match
    c) What skills need work during training

At the end of a day, you should always take a few minutes to review your performance. There may have been one shot in the match that constantly let you down, and you need to work on that during training. It may be that you failed to exercise mental toughness, or even that your opponent was simply 'too good'.

I have a small A5 sheet of paper that I write on after every match I play. If I have multiple matches in a single day, I complete all the forms that same evening. The form contains the above three questions, plus:

    i) Rate your game out of 10
    ii) Rate your opponent's game out of 10
    iii) Rate your mental toughness out of 10
    iv) Rate your preparation out of 10
    v) Rate your concentration out of 10
    vi) Any other comments or notes

To be satisfied with my match performance, I must score at least 40 points out of 50. 30 of the 50 points are practical and 20 of the 50 points are mental. The opponent's score also counts toward the total, as an opponent who plays well must be considered in your overall assessment of the match.

Below are two examples of a performance review. The first card was a loss, while the second card was a win.

2018 World Champion of Champions

October 2018 vs Zimbabwe

Score: LOSS 6-8 / 11-2 / 2-3

a) What you could have done better

Hydrated better during the game and taken the mat on the first end of the tie-break after winning the toss

b) What you learnt from the match

Covering the re-spot may seem like the right decision at the time, but when behind in a set, I should focus more on taking chances and going for larger counts instead of just winning ends

c) What skills need work during training
My backhand runner and short ends with the mat up the green
i) Rate your game out of 10: 7
ii) Rate your opponent's game out of 10: 7
iii) Rate your mental toughness out of 10: **8**
iv) Rate your preparation out of 10: **10**
v) Rate your concentration out of 10: **9**
SCORE: 41/50 - SATISFACTORY

Comments: Drew well on my favourite length of ditch to ditch. Opponent drove me off the green in the first set, sinking the jack in the ditch five times. Only one hand of the rink was playable, and often there was no way to the buried jack except on the hard hand. Scored 19 shots to 13 in the match but lost the tie-break. Dropped three shots on the first end of the tie-break after choosing to give the mat away instead of keeping it, after winning the toss. This was a mistake, as the change of length by my opponent disrupted my draw consistency from the second set. Maybe consider taking the mat in the tie-break next time I win the toss, if I have won the second set.

2019 World Champion of Champions
October 2019 v Singapore
Score: WIN 13-4 / 11-2
a) What you could have done better
My concentration waivered throughout the game. My jack rolling was inconsistent

b) What you learnt from the match

Morning matches suffer from heavy dew at this venue and after the roll-up, the moisture comes up and the green loses pace instantly

c) What skills need work during training

Jack rolling

i) Rate your game out of 10: **5**
ii) Rate your opponent's game out of 10: **3**
iii) Rate your mental toughness out of 10: **7**
iv) Rate your preparation out of 10: **10**
v) Rate your concentration out of 10: **5**

SCORE: 30/50 - UNSATISFACTORY

<u>Comments</u>: Being the first game of the event, I was very scratchy. My opponent was inexperienced and unfamiliar with green speeds above 10 seconds. I expect to play better as the tournament progresses, but there was no excuse for inconsistent concentration and lapses in mental toughness. If I want to make the finals of this event, I need to increase my mental application, better my attitude, and the good bowls will follow.

Interestingly, a satisfactory performance came during a loss, while an unsatisfactory performance was the outcome of a win. The result should never impact your performance review. You should analyse your performance on your key indicators, setting aside the result for the time being. The lessons of failure and managing success are what deals with the result.

Each sheet takes less than five minutes to complete and it is a great way of remembering your opponent, the score and what you learnt from a previous encounter. Friends will often joke that I remember the scores from every match I ever played. This is partly true, but only because I have performance sheets dating back twelve years, still on file.

Considering all the information above, you need to realise that 20 points can be achieved almost every time, simply by ensuring your concentration and mental toughness are at the level they should be. The graphs of my performances over the past six years show that my mental toughness has improved out of sight. I used to accept 30 points as a satisfactory performance, but not long after, chose to increase the challenge and re-set the bar to 40 points. You can adjust your own target as necessary.

Reviewing your own performance is a way of defining what adjustments need to be made to your training schedule. 40% of the score in a performance review relates specifically to your mental application, so if you concentrate well and ensure your mental toughness is sharp, you are half-way to a satisfactory performance.

CHAPTER 33

Selection

In team sport, selection is always a factor. Selection is defined as the action of carefully choosing someone, as being the best, or most suitable.

Most bowlers at club level are subject to pennant selection by their selection committee. These committees are generally formed at a club Annual General Meeting (the meeting), after nominations for the roles have been received in advance. Sometimes, a selector or number of selectors, may be accepted from the floor at the meeting. Once formed, a committee will generally appoint a chairman, who takes on the role of 'Chairman of Selectors'. As well as club selectors, there are also Regional or Zone selectors, State selectors and National selectors. Every bowler at one point or another will be subject to selection throughout their career.

Selection is a two-way street. At times you may be subject to selection, while other times you may be the one selecting. It is important to understand the role you play in each of these situations.

The Role of a Selector

Before you consider taking on the role of a selector within your club (or beyond), you should carefully consider whether you are a good fit for the job. Selectors can 'make or break' a bowling club in many respects. Too many unjustifiable mistakes can lose the confidence of the members, result in dismissal, or even worse, the loss of members to other clubs. Selection is a tough job. If you enter the role trying to please everyone, you will fail.

I have identified 10 traits that make a good selector:
- Always use the adult ego
- Always tell the truth
- Be respectful to those you select and those you work with
- Stay calm and listen to people
- Allow meetings to discuss player grievances
- Give feedback to players as required
- Give valid reasons to those you have dropped or omitted
- Suggest ideas or methods to those you have dropped or omitted

- Admit when you are wrong and be clear on how you will rectify it
- Be clear with your message and never use ulterior conversation

All the above points are common sense, designed to gain and retain the trust and faith of those you are selecting.

Being involved in selection for a majority of the past 15 years, I have dealt with many complaints and grievances. Mind you, sometimes I have had to admit my decision was wrong and propose a way to rectify the mistake.

As a selector, I am always willing to listen to what an aggrieved person has to say, despite how inaccurate their objections may be. Sometimes a complainant brings an adult ego into the meeting, but generally a child ego arrives. Once they have stated their case, I will always respond with the truth. You may fear offending a player with what you say, but if constructed carefully, you can respond truthfully, and as an adult. You must always answer the questions, provide feedback, and suggest ideas or methods, that may open the opportunity for that player moving forward. Although a player may leave a meeting disgruntled, telling the truth will resonate with the player once their emotions have been grounded. They are more likely to respect you for being truthful, than if you were to use ulterior conversation or lies.

As Chairman of Selectors, I once dealt with a hostile complaint from an aggrieved member. The member requested a meeting with the selection panel, which I of course accepted. The individual was Chairman of the Selectors of our club in the previous year and chose not to re-nominate for selection. The basis of the complaint was that he had been separated from playing with his spouse, who he had selected as his third for the previous season. On providing exact reasons why the panel decided to make the separation, as well as including clear reasons why this individual was not selected to skip, I was accused of nepotism as he stormed out of the room. The same member chose to clear from the club, just months after holding the selection reigns. Sometimes no matter how well you listen, how truthful you are, or how politely you respond to a complaint, you can't help them being a condescending idiot!

Being Subject to Selection

When subject to selection, you have rights.

If you are ever confused, disgruntled, upset, or disappointed in a selection decision, you should request feedback from the selection committee. The best way to have your questions answered, is to request a meeting with the selectors.

If you go to a meeting with a selection committee, always be prepared. I can guarantee you that a selection committee will have anticipated your questions and prepared accordingly themselves. Before you make accusations or stake claim to your position, ensure you have the evidence to support your arguments. A good selection panel will answer your questions, provide valid reasons for your omission or change, and suggest ideas or ways you can get your position back. An honest panel will also admit any wrongdoing by you and rectify it as soon as possible.

When attending a meeting of the selectors, you should always enter with an adult ego. The best way to argue your case is to be honest, professional and to remain calm. If you can do this, a selection panel is more likely to treat your complaint with sincerity and empathy. Walking into a selection meeting with a 'bee in your bonnet', flustered, angry, and grumpy, will not only make you appear silly, but probably result in your complaint being dismissed by the panel.

Always make the effort to listen to what the selectors have to say. They may have good reason for making a change and will probably give you a solution or ideas on how you can regain your spot moving forward. You should leave the meeting with clear knowledge on what you need to do to regain your position.

Selectors who rely on their authority, without giving relative feedback and valid reasons for their decisions, should not be selectors.

Then again, after reviewing the 'National Team Selection Policy' published by Bowls Australia on their website, and noting the indefensible position of the athletes, maybe my views on selection are wrong.

CHAPTER 34

Form

One of the most misunderstood terms in the sporting world is 'form'. In bowls, your form is constantly judged by selectors, coaches, team leaders and media. Sometimes they are so critical, it has serious and lasting effects on your career.

My theory on form decides that if you train efficiently, give your best in every match, think positively, and have solid levels of self-belief, then you are **always** in form. Form is an opinion and the only opinion that counts, is yours. Form is a self-perceived notion and is not determined by any person other than you. You may receive constructive feedback or advice on a performance that you should take onboard, but do not let it negate your attitude. As like momentum, form is simply the ebbs and flows of your bowling career. Allowing form to influence your decision making can distract you from your goals and desired results.

Factors that Determine Form

Being in form is determined by three key elements:
1) Training efficiently
2) Doing your best
3) Self-belief

Training Efficiently

If you believe you are religiously following your training regime and are not getting the results you expect, then you may conclude that you are 'out of form'. Remember that you decide whether you are in form, not your results. You may need to visit your training schedule and make some minor adjustments. If you have identified any new weakness, whether physical or mental, you may need to devote extra training time to it. Having a weakness does not mean you are out of form; it is merely an identification of something you can work on to improve your overall performance.

Doing Your Best

If your preparation is perfect and you give your best in a match, then the result will take care of itself. The result is always 'on the day', and sometimes anything can happen. You can run into an opponent who plays better, you can have a disappointing performance, or a mixture of both. Winning a match may seem the most important factor, but the result should never change your attitude on form. I have often said that one performance does not make a career. There will be matches where you play extremely well and others, where no matter how hard you try, you can't seem to do anything right. So long as you enter a match with the right frame of mind, stay mentally strong, and do your best with every shot you play, then you must accept that you did your best. It may be the rub of the green that decides who wins and who loses, but that's just bowls.

<u>Self-Belief</u>

If you allow form to influence your mental toughness, then your level of self-belief is questionable. The negative thought of being out of form will directly affect your level of confidence. It is possible that you enter a match resigned to defeat, accepting the result before it has happened.

Mirage Form

Remember when we discussed the idea of 'mirage confidence' and how the act of pretending you are confident (even when you feel down on confidence) can often positively change your level of confidence? The same applies here with form.

Despite how awful you feel on the green during a match, continue to stand tall, remove negative thoughts, and increase positive thoughts. If you are finding it difficult to remove negative thoughts, constantly remind yourself that you are in form. Say to yourself, "I am in form. I always have been, and I always will be". Repetition of this statement can push out any negative thoughts. This skill has the potential to reverse a tough situation and increase your chances of winning the match. The longer you pretend to be in form, the more chance you will believe it. Positive thoughts will attract a positive outcome.

Always in Form

As simple as it sounds, if form is determined by efficient training, giving it your best, and believing in yourself, then you may as well get used to the idea of always being in form.

Take it from me. If you can truly look yourself in the mirror and convince yourself that you could not be training better, are confident, believe in yourself, and that you are always in good form, then you always will be.

Even a string of poor results or sub-standard performances should not detract you from this idea. Minor adjustments may need to be made to your training program or preparation to help improve your performance, but never accept being out of form. Once you start blaming results on poor form, you have become a victim and surrendered to the persecutor. Face your challenges and find a way to overcome them. If you take on this attitude, then you will never be out form.

PART H

Skills & Character

CHAPTER 35

Leadership

Leadership is not something you are born with, despite what you may have heard. Leadership can be instilled in your brain from an early age and the ability to lead is closely correlated with the way you were brought up. Although a factor, your upbringing does not officially decide whether you can be a leader or not.

Leadership can be taught, allowing anyone to become a leader. Leadership is an attitude choice. Some of us are too shy to want to lead, while others believe they don't have the necessary skills. Leadership is a trait that forms part of your overall character.

I have developed a list of ten key qualities of good leadership. Whether you lead a team now or choose to lead a team in the future, understanding and applying these ten techniques will improve your leadership skills.

1) The ability to inspire others

As a leader, you must have the ability to inspire others. Other people will place a faith and trust in you as a leader and you need to know what to say (or what to do) to inspire them. You are the one responsible for lifting a team that is flat or shows a lack of interest.

2) Communication

You may be aware of what you feel as a leader, but how you communicate your thoughts can often be critical. Every human is different and while some may react positively to your message, others may be offended.

Also, you may be clear on what you want to achieve as a leader, but make sure your team-mates know your goals. If they are clearly aware of what you want to achieve, then they can marry their own goals to suit that of their leader. This will create team goal congruence.

3) Confidence

Always demonstrate a confident approach, even when you are not feeling confident yourself. The team will look to you in troublesome times and by displaying a confident attitude, your aura will feed through to them. Demonstrating supreme and perseverant confidence always, will ensure your team never gives up.

4) Positivity

A positive leader will encourage their team to work harder. A good split between serious training and team bonding will create a positive team culture. Your positivity could be the reason why team-mates train an extra hour a week, or why your team continually gets over the line in the close matches.

5) Delegation

In a team environment, you cannot do everything yourself. Once your message is clear to the players, you need to place faith in their ability to execute the game plan. You may intervene from time to time to assist, but you must trust the team and their individual decisions. In pennant, you must also have faith and trust in the skippers who lead other rinks.

6) Honesty

Be ethical and honest with your team. There is no need to beat around the bush if times are hard, and sometimes an honest and frank discussion will separate the supporters from the rogues. If you are honest about what you communicate, then you will have no regrets as a leader. Some of your team may disagree with your thoughts or theories, but they will always have respect for an honest leader.

7) Commitment

Lead by example and be the team mentor. You are the one everyone looks up to, so the example you set must be at the very highest level. Everything you do will attach to your team-mates, so always think carefully about your actions.

You may make mistakes from time to time, so identify them, acknowledge them for what they are and eliminate them. Discussing your flaws or mistakes with team-mates is not a sign of weakness so long as they trust and respect you. Your dedication gains the respect of a team, so admitting fault will only increase trust among the group.

8) Intuition

Having the ability to see the future is left to Super-Heroes. Although you cannot see the future, you need an intuition or 'gut feel' for what is to come. A leader will identify when a team talk is needed or when an adjustment to the game plan is required, before it is too late. Experience will provide the leader with a sixth sense that can set the way for team success. You will not always be right, but over time, your strike-rate will improve.

9) Creativity

A good leader is creative. With an attitude of 'think outside the square', a leader can achieve more from their players than the ability they have.

I once had my team train corner-to-corner on a Tuesday night and on a football oval the same Thursday night. We were expecting a very damp and ultra-slow track for an away pennant match that Saturday. As our green ran constantly above 17 seconds, the creative training was designed to take the shock factor out of the expected dead track. It worked; we won comfortably.

10) <u>Authority</u>
A leader will have to make difficult decisions involving players and teams. A good leader will already have the trust and faith of their team, which means that any authority delivered will be respected and appreciated.

If new in a leadership role, you should tread very carefully with authority. You may not have earnt the respect of your teammates yet, so applying too much authority can create objections, division, and dissent.

My ten qualities of good leadership work most effectively when coupled with the right style of leadership. All great leaders in sport have the skill to change their leadership style when appropriate. You may not always get it right, but acknowledging mistakes will enhance your experience.

There are seven main types of leadership. Like management, choosing the right style impacts the performance of your subordinates. If you get it right, the response of your team will be positive and constructive. It is important you understand each style and when to apply it.

1) Autocratic

An autocratic leader rules the team with an iron fist. They make all the decisions with little or no input from others and command the team in all facets. Historically, this dictator type of leadership had massive followings, but in a modern society, the role of an autocratic leader is somewhat diminished.

You may be required to exercise autocratic leadership from time to time. It is especially beneficial when dealing with inexperienced team-mates, or when a decision must be made immediately.

2) Authoritarian

An authoritarian ruler makes most of the decisions for a team but also provides clear explanations for each decision. Some input is taken onboard from team-mates, but generally the authoritarian leader will set the path to success or failure. They are the visionary who decides the direction of a team, helping guide a team to common goals.

This style of leadership is common among skippers and coaches. To be successful as an authoritarian leader, you must be clear on your own visions and your visions for the team. If used effectively, this style of leadership can inspire goal congruence and a common culture. Only a leader with established credibility should attempt an authoritarian role.

3) <u>Observation</u>

An observation leader is a team mentor with a 'do as I do' attitude. They are a leader who sets the example for everyone else, inspiring others to follow in their shoes. This style is especially tough to control, as any leadership mistakes or flaws can be duplicated by a team. Observation leaders must be extremely well behaved, have a sound attitude and excellent body language.

This style of leadership is especially influential with new bowlers or junior bowlers. It is a practical approach to leadership where inexperienced or new bowlers can develop guidance through your actions.

4) <u>Democratic</u>

A democratic leader is one who seeks the opinions and thoughts of others before making any decision. Democracy is a huge part of modern-day leadership, but easily the most difficult strategy to succeed. A democratic leader will make some team-mates extremely happy while others will feel left out or isolated. You cannot please everyone, so only use this style of leadership during one-on-one interactions. That way, you only have the opinion or thought of one other person, making it easier for you to make decisions.

If a democratic leader attempts to please everyone, they will almost certainly fail. In politics, a democratic leader is only interested in pleasing the majority. For this reason, I believe democratic leadership has no place in team sport. Any leadership style that encourages individual opinions in a team environment, is more likely to instigate division, conflict, and dissention rather than a positive culture.

5) Considerate
A considerate leader is one who develops idea and suggests them to a team, attempting to convince them to agree. This style is somewhat ulterior, where the leader will ask team-mates to consider numerous situations or schemes, all designed to direct the team in one specific direction. When a majority disagree with the suggestion, the leader divulges a modified suggestion with the same idea in mind, as an attempt to increase following.

Considerate leadership is most appropriate to the introduction of change. Human nature tells you that most individuals feel an adversity to change. If the change is important to your coaching or leadership, it is feasible that considerate leadership can convince your team that the change is productive.

6) Collaborative
A collaborative leader is one who gets up close and personal with each member of a team. They take notes of the emotional needs and wants of a team-member, attempting to form a relationship of trust and respect on an individual level. They believe that people come first, and any decisions they make are influenced by the prerequisites of each individual in the team.

This style of leadership is built on a foundation of truth. If you choose to exercise this style you must never tell a lie, as if discovered, the individual relationship can become hostile and evaporate. This style is dangerous as it is almost impossible to please everyone, meaning you often compromise. By compromising, you lose control and your leadership is effectively operated by the individuals within your team.

7) <u>Free-Reign</u>

A free-reign leadership style places high levels of trust on each member of a team. The style assumes that team-mates are so highly skilled, that they can make all decisions without any influence from their leader. A leader has little oversight and supervision of the team, allowing them to exercise their own thoughts and judgement.

Team sport holds no place for this leadership style. Allowing individuals of a team to drift in their own direction can break the foundations of team culture and team goals. An individual may put their own opinions ahead of team values, resulting in goal incongruence.

Leadership is not for the faint-hearted. By appropriately applying a leadership style with the ten techniques of good leadership, you can become a successful leader. A leader will live and die by the sword, but the rewards of leading a team to triumph will always outweigh any failures along the way.

Once a team believes in your approach, your decisions will resonate. Your influence decides whether a team celebrates the joy of victory, or suffers an agonising defeat.

CHAPTER 36

Personal Limits

As simple as is sounds, understanding your personal limits, is widely ignored in the bowling community. Many refuse to understand their restrictions and limits and attempt to apply ad-hoc and rash strategies to their game. Similarly, skippers and team leaders fail to understand the limitations of the individuals in their team, and subsequently drive goals that are impossible to achieve.

If you are limited physically, whether by age or disability, you, your skipper, your coach, and all other team leaders need to be aware of your restriction. Some limitations are more obvious than others. For example, trying to play a drive beyond your own natural and physical capability is not only likely to be unsuccessful, it is dangerous and irresponsible.

Your limits are not necessarily your weaknesses. You can adjust your training to cater for weakness. Your limits are what you physically cannot do.

It is difficult for some lawn bowlers to swallow their pride and accept physical limits. There are still a large group who choose to 'dump' bowls from around their hip, rather than invest in a bowling arm. A bad back, severe arthritis, weight issues and age, are all physical limitations that some refuse to accept.

By identifying the limits of you and your team, you can create a modified game plan. This tailored game plan will reduce ignorance on shot selection and tactics and construct the most appropriate scheme to win. If you are not the skipper, make them fully aware of your limitations so that they can incorporate them into their strategy. A good skipper will take note of these limitations and adjust their game plan accordingly.

As an example, if you cannot physically bowl on your backhand due to a disability or pain, failing to make your skipper aware of this limitation will see you called to play backhand shots for around half of the match. If your skipper is aware prior to the match starting, they can make a conscious effort to keep you on your forehand side as much as possible. The acceptance and relay of your limitation will not only make you feel more comfortable about the match but will result in a better performance. A better performance will please you, your skipper and the rest of your team-mates.

Attempting to out-do yourself and achieve physical impossibilities increases the likelihood of injury. Fully understand your limits and stick to your capabilities. Although these limits can reduce your shot play, you are more likely to achieve a better performance.

In my 20's I was known to have one of the quickest and most accurate drive shots in the country. In 2015 I slipped on a wet mat in Perth while attempting a drive and dislocated a vertebra in my neck. This injury resulted in multiple physiotherapy and chiropractic sessions and limited me from playing my drive. I acknowledged this limitation and spent hours on the training track developing a slower and more comfortable weighted shot. By understanding this limitation, I was able to modify my game plan accordingly. Even though my range of shots had decreased, I conditioned myself to ignore the option of a full-blooded drive, so when the shot became an option, I dismissed it immediately due to my limitation.

Five years later my neck had fully recovered, and the drive shot was re-introduced to my game plan. Had I not 'put the cue in the rack' for those years, it is probable that more neck damage would have occurred, and the likelihood of a full recovery would have been next to zero.

CHAPTER 37

Match Tempo

Match tempo, or speed at which a match progresses, can often have a bearing on the final score or outcome. Adjusting the match tempo can put a match on your terms, allowing you to potentially regain control that may have been lost. Although involving a level of gamesmanship, influencing the match tempo can deter you from 'going through the motions' and accepting defeat.

When it comes to match tempo, you need to understand two important points:
 1) You control match tempo by how fast or slow you play
 2) Regardless of the speed of your opponent, play the tempo which best suits you

Effective use of match tempo techniques can change the pattern of a game and consciously affect the result. It could make you slow down, concentrate, and play at a higher level. It could also frustrate your opponent, influence their performance, and distract their concentration. In its finest form, match tempo will do both.

I am first to admit that I apply match tempo techniques when I believe they can increase my chances winning a match. With experience, you too can apply certain techniques to help you through a tough match. Not everyone plays well in every match they play, so controlling match tempo will keep the game on your terms, help you stay in your comfort zone, and increase your chances of winning. In events such as State or National Championships, you need to win an extraordinary amount of consecutive games. If every match is played on your terms, then you expand the likelihood of stringing multiple wins together.

It is common knowledge that younger bowlers play a lot quicker than middle-aged and older bowlers. They like to keep the game moving fast, get involved with every shot and are often chopping at your heels awaiting their turn.

Slower players are never fussed by how fast their opponent plays. They take their time and go through a deliberate and specific routine before every shot. The game is generally played on their terms.

I specifically enjoy playing against players who constantly play at a fast tempo. Often when I go and look at the head, or when

I step back off the mat after being distracted in my normal routine, I can hear sniggering and groans from my opposition. Their impatience can cause frustration, distract them, and even affect their level of performance. Their reaction should never phase you or encourage you to speed up. Keep the game on your terms and play at the speed that is most comfortable to you.

If you are a naturally fast-moving player, changing the match tempo can be a difficult proposition. If the scoreboard is against you or your opponent is clearly on top, you need to slow the tempo of the match, find some time to assess the situation, and devise a plan to get back into the match.

To buy some time, and potentially upset the tempo of an opponent playing well, take the following into account:

a) Always go through your normal and specific routine for each delivery, no matter how fast or slow you are (extremely important)

b) If your opponent walks to the head, follow them, and wait until their bowl has come to rest before you walk back to play yours

c) Always ask questions of the marker in singles, or one of your players in a team game, even if you know what the answer will be. If you are confident of holding shot, it can add insult to injury for an opponent to also get confirmation of the position from the other end of the green

d) If your opponent is painfully slow, then attempt to play slower than they are. Funnily enough, this can often result in a slow playing opponent rushing their own shots, trying to get match tempo back on their terms

e) Walk to the head at times when you are holding shot and need to cover. Look at all angles of contact, the re-spot if appropriate, and any other positions of cover that yield the most danger. Then, walk back up the green, apply your normal routine and delivery and execute the shot of choice. This delay tactic increases the time an opponent realises they are down on the head, and despite the score, can invite a poor decision or a rushed mistake

Tempo must be decided by you. If you are unable to get the game on your own terms, then slowing down your speed of play is probably the solution.

The scoreboard can affect the speed of your play. If behind, slow down and be more deliberate with decision making and shot selection. Concentrate on going through your routine with each individual bowl and remain in the perseverance level of confidence. If you are in front and your opponent continues to play fast, do not attempt to slow the game down in any way. Fast players will often get even faster when they are behind, going through the motions until the match concludes.

Match tempo has a clear gamesmanship aspect. One thing is for certain though, it is a quality skill to have. It can often dig you out of a hole, or help you stumble over the line in a close match.

CHAPTER 38

Exercise & Fitness

As strange as it sounds, exercise and general fitness form an integral part of improving your game of bowls. Over the last decade, high performance has come to prominence, especially at the elite level. In Australia, bowlers who are selected into the National Squad are required to participate in the high-performance program. Part of this program includes regular exercise and fitness.

Exercise is an attitude choice. If you want to be fitter and healthier, you need to make the choice to do so.

Exercise is widely known to have many benefits, including but not limited to:
- Strengthening your bones and muscles
- Improving your mood and mental health
- Helping control your weight

- Lowering your risk of disease
- Prolonging your life

I have been the culprit of poor fitness levels for many years. My attitude was ignorant to all types of exercise, completely withdrawing it from my program. It was not until my endurance was tested in long events such as the Victorian Open, that I realised this area of my game needed more attention. I am not getting any younger, so my fitness had to become a priority. I didn't have to go as far as lifting weights at the gym, or swimming 30 laps at the local pool, but I did have to find a way to increase my endurance.

I am not a professional trainer or physiotherapist, so will steer clear of providing specific advice on exercise and fitness. Just remember that everyone is different, and your fitness regime needs to be tailored to your specific needs and requirements.

Walking formed an important part of my fitness training. Instead of driving my car short distances, I started walking. I also increased my training hours, purposely trying to build-up my endurance.

Bowls itself is great exercise as it involves minor weight-lifting, walking, and strengthening of your core. The repetitive action of a bowls delivery will not only build core strength, but also improve your balance and flexibility.

On a personal note, I found plyometrics (jump training) to be beneficial as it improved my balance, flexibility, core strength and overall level of fitness. I was introduced to this style of training after breaking my ankle, as a way of strengthening a weak joint. I also enjoy it, making me more likely to do it regularly.

Taking all the above into account, I have learnt a few tips that have proven useful to me during a match, and later, in recovery. Although very basic ideas, the increase in my endurance has been very noticeable:

- Lightly stretch before and after a match as this increases blood circulation, enables better flexibility, and may prevent injury

- After a long day on the green, have a hot and cold shower i.e. turn the water from hot to cold every few seconds. This also improves blood circulation and has other benefits such as pain relief and reduction of any inflammation

- Keep your fluids up to reduce the likelihood of cramps and a loss in concentration. You should alternate between sports drinks and water to ensure the sodium level in your body is at normal levels

These three handy tips will help you get through long and tough matches, as well as allowing you to have a comfortable night's sleep. If you can at least follow these three tips, you are more likely to wake up relaxed, fresh, and fit for another day of bowls. This is especially important if you need to bowl multiple days in a row.

You should consult your local gym, personal trainer, or physiotherapist for specific exercises you can undertake to help your bowls. Not only will your bowls experience be more pleasurable, but you will also reap the other known benefits of exercise.

CHAPTER 39

Sportsmanship & Respect

Coming across as a bad sport, will result in you being labelled 'exactly that' for an eternity in lawn bowls. From your very first day on the green, you need to understand the quality of sportsmanship and respect towards your team-mates, spectators, umpires, equipment, and most importantly, your opposition.

Sportsmanship is defined as the fair and generous treatment of others, especially during a match. In a bowling sense, respect in defined as due regard for the feelings, wishes and rights of others, both during a match, and off the green.

Without doubt, I have experienced many acts of anger and frustration in my career, that could easily brand me as a 'bad sport'. As my experience grew, I began to learn the importance of sportsmanship and respect.

Displaying sportsmanship and respect is an attitude choice. You can condition yourself to be a better sport. You could instrumentally reward yourself for a string of sportsmanlike displays, while penalising yourself anytime you disrespect equipment, bowlers, or officials. Further, you could observe the sportsmanship of a mentor, taking note of their grace, respect, and skill under pressure. Conditioning can teach you to become a good sport.

I have conditioned myself many times over the years, after some disrespectful acts of post-game rage and anger. Although acting with sportsmanship and respect on the green, I have disrespected opponents and equipment after a loss. If I have learnt anything over time through my mistakes, it is that these acts will have a more profound impact on your career than any loss could ever have. From time to time, we all make mistakes. You must clear your conscience by apologising sincerely, acknowledging your mistake, confirming it will not happen again, and ask for forgiveness.

Gamesmanship

There is a key difference between gamesmanship and sportsmanship.

Gamesmanship involves incorporating methods and tactics to win, that border on unethical behaviour. It is essentially doing everything you can within the rules to win a match. If you choose to use gamesmanship as a tactic, you must be calculated and subtle. Poor use could offend and disrespect your opposition, increasing their devotion and passion to beat you.

Dealing with Bad Sports

On the green, a bowler must learn to **never** comment negatively on an opponent's bowl, or to cheer or support their own bad bowls that fluke good results. It might sound basic on paper, but a lot of bowlers out there do not get the concept. If you make fun of an opposition bowl or clap and cheer flukes, you are a bad sport.

I have met some awfully bad sports in my time. Their actions made me realise how stupid I must have looked when doing similar things. Over the past decade, I have worked hard on my sportsmanship and respect. It certainly isn't perfect, but it is a massive improvement on the past.

Pennant competition generally involves the worst level of sportsmanship. Even though it exists in other matches like singles, social bowls or tournaments, some clubs will do anything to win a pennant match. Bad sportsmanship brands the club for life, making them a target for other teams.

Just because you may play against a team of 'sledgers' or 'bad sports', does not mean you have to stoop to their level. Reacting to their poor sportsmanship is exactly what they want you to do. They throw out a baited hook, waiting for someone to bite. Once you bite, you are distracted from the team's goals and objectives and have fallen victim to the stupidity of your opposition. Who is the stupid one now? Ignoring an unsportsmanlike opposition achieves much more than a reaction.

Don't find yourself intimidated or upset by a 'win at all costs' opposition. It is likely they fear your skill and quality, believing they must do more than play well to get over the line. You are a threat to them, and they want to derail your concentration. As a threat or target, you should let the bowls do the talking, and see who reigns supreme at the end.

He who laughs last, laughs longest!

CONCLUSION

Congratulations on reaching the end of *In the Zone II – Secrets of a World Champ*. It is now time to put the theory into practice. At any time, you can pick up this book and re-read any section that is relevant to you.

Once you have a grasp on the six critical theories of mental toughness, you can apply them to any chapter in this book. These critical theories should set the foundation of developing your mental toughness. A failure to understand these critical sections will mean other chapters do not have the influence and intent they were written for.

You must understand the concept of gaining a desired result and how to reach this result through setting goals, understanding the process, and following a routine.

You need to be completely familiar with victim theory, the drama triangle, and the empowerment dynamic. You need to be clear on the roles of a victim, creator, challenger, persecutor, rescuer, and coach. These roles are filtered through the whole book, and your understanding of each role will help you process and implement each chapter successfully.

The Law of Attraction may be confronting and difficult to comprehend at first, but constant re-reading will engrave this theory firmly on your mind. The three laws have become a religion for me, and I use them every day. If you don't 'get it' or 'feel it', that is perfectly okay. It is a theory that did wonders for me, and not sharing it with you would let me believe the book was incomplete.

Conditioning is an amazing process, where you can make an attitude choice to believe in anything you want, and to teach yourself anything you choose to. Through conditioning, you are unable to make excuses for poor behaviour or a bad attitude. You now have the tool to overcome negative traits and rebuild your character from the bottom-up.

Courage teaches you to confront your fears and how to overcome them. A courageous bowler has skill and grace under pressure, will never give up, and will make you earn every shot you get. A courageous bowler is not lucky when they win a close game; they deserve it.

Most things in bowls are a choice. You need to make the willpower choices to overcome unwanted thoughts, emotions, and temptations. You must have the ability to make mindful choices without relying on impulse or outside influences.

Over time, these six critical theories will be etched into your game permanently. The positive change in your performance and results will be evident almost immediately. If these theories are shown to improve your game (and I know they will), then you are likely to attach yourself to many sections of this book. I want you to treat it as your 'bowling bible'. Whenever things get tough and you feel like you need a divine intervention, just remind yourself that nothing is impossible to fix. Somewhere in this book lies your answer.

You will still make mistakes from time-to-time, but don't beat yourself up over it. Part of the learning process is to identify these errors and understand how to rectify them moving forward. This book covers every mental mistake a bowler can make. Look up the topic relevant to your mistake, re-read it and remind yourself of how to avoid that mistake moving forward, or how to better deal with it on the green next time.

Be honest with yourself, do the work, and get your game to a better place. If I can become a World Champion, even with my mental deficiencies, then anything is possible for you too.

The End

My final piece of advice is something I tell new bowlers when they have their first pleasurable experience of our great sport. I look them in the eye and tell them that the only way to genuinely enjoy lawn bowls, is if you believe in this mantra:

> *"Never play bowls to prove other people wrong. Always play to prove yourself right".*

In the end, all that matters, is what you believe!

ABOUT THE AUTHOR

Lee Schraner is a former Australian International representative and a World Champion of Champions Singles Gold and Bronze Medallist. He has 26 years of lawn bowling experience, and 18 years of coaching experience.

On beginning his coaching career, Lee began keeping notes on a wide variety of topics. Many of these subjects provided the basis for the release of *"In the Zone – Mental Toughness in Lawn Bowls"* in 2014.

Although not qualified in any aspect of psychology, his theories have been tested, modified, and applied to his match play and coaching for many years.

Lee played only one official test match for Australia in 2010 before being omitted from the Australian squad prior to the 2010 Commonwealth Games in Delhi, India.

He has represented Australia at Under 25 level on 12 occasions and played 28 games for Australia at the World Champion of Champions Singles event in 2018 and 2019. In total, he has represented Australia 41 times.

Lee lost just 6 of his 41 matches in Australian colours and just 2 of his 31 singles matches, ending his career with an overall 84% International win percentage and an unbelievable 94% win record in singles.

Today, Lee lives in Spring Gully, a leafy urban area just outside of Bendigo in Victoria. He still has goals of representing his beloved State of Victoria, even after 302 Interstate test matches. At 38 years of age, Lee is retired from International Representation and is devoting more of his time to coaching, writing, and mentoring.

He still struggles at times with mental illness and continues to work on his mental toughness every day.

COACHING HISTORY

Bendigo East Bowling Club
Head Coach Seasons: 2018/19, 2019/20, 2020/21

Rosny Park Bowling Club
Head Coach Seasons: 2016/2017, 2017/2018

Glenorchy-Rodman Bowling Club
Head Coach Seasons: 2014/2015

Brunswick Bowling Club
Co-Opted Coach Seasons: 2011/2012, 2012/2013

Brighton Bowling & Sporting Clubs Inc
Assistant Coach Seasons: 2009/2010, 2010/2011, 2011/2012, 2012/2013

Karingal Bowling Club
Head Coach Seasons: 2007/2008, 2008/2009

Bundoora RSL Bowling Club
Finals Coaching Co-Ordinator: 2002/2003
Head Coach Seasons: 2003/2004, 2004/2005, 2005/2006, 2006/2007

MAJOR ACHIEVEMENTS

International Achievements – World Title Medals
- 2019 World Champion of Champions Singles GOLD Medal
- 2018 World Champion of Champions Singles BRONZE Medal

International Representation
- Retired 2019 after omission from the Australian Emerging Squad
- Australian Emerging Squad 2018-2019

- Australian Representative #132 (One representative match)
- Australian Squad 2008-2010
- Australian Under 25 Representative v New Zealand 2006 & 2007 (12 representative matches)

Australian Rankings Achievements
- Ranked in the Top #5 in Australia from 2010-2020 (10 years, 2 months)
- Australian #1 ranked bowler (September 2018 - April 2019)

National Level Gold Medals / National Titles (15)
- 2019 Australian Fours GOLD Medal with Brad Johns, Josh Appleyard & Rob McMullen
- 2018 Australian Champion of Champions Singles GOLD Medal
- 2018 Victorian Open Singles GOLD Medal
- 2017 Australian Champion of Champions GOLD Medal
- 2017 Victorian Open VIC MEDAL for best performed player at the open
- 2017 Australian Masters Games Pairs GOLD Medal with Mark Nitz
- 2017 Australian Masters Games Triples GOLD Medal with Rick Ormerod & Deb O'Donnell
- 2017 Victorian Open Triples GOLD Medal with Brad Marron & Dylan Filuk

- 2017 Victorian Open Mixed Pairs GOLD Medal
with Gayle Edwards
- 2016 Victorian Open Pairs GOLD Medal
with Brad Marron
- 2012 Victorian Open Pairs GOLD Medal
with Aaron Wilson
- 2012 Victorian Open Mixed Pairs GOLD Medal
with Gayle Edwards
- 2011 Australian Open Pairs GOLD Medal
with Neville Rodda
- 2009 Queensland Open Triples GOLD Medal
with Dylan Fisher & Todd Simmons
- 2006 Victorian Grand Prix Triples GOLD Medal
with Joel Simmonds & Paul Dorgan

State Championships (18)
- State Fours Champion (2) 2019 TAS & 2016 TAS
- State Singles Champion (2) 2018 TAS & 2011 VIC
- State Champion of Champions Singles (6) 2018 TAS, 2017 TAS, 2013 VIC, 2011 VIC, 2009 VIC & 2008 VIC
- State Pairs Champion (2) 2016 TAS & 2007 VIC
- State Triples Champion (2) 2018 TAS & 2017 TAS
- Under 30 Singles Champion (3) 2006 VIC, 2003 VIC & 2001 VIC
- VSSSA Secondary Schools Fours Champion (1) 1997 VIC

State Representation (302)
- Tasmanian Squad 2014 – 2019 (91 games)
- Victorian Squad 2004 – 2013 (206 games);
2019 – current (5 games)

Regional / Zone Championships (43)
- Regional Singles Champion (6) 2020, 2018, 2017, 2015, 2014 & 2011
- Regional Champion of Champions Singles (8) 2018, 2017, 2013, 2011, 2009, 2008, 2006 & 2004
- Regional Under 30 Singles Champion (7) 2008, 2007, 2006, 2005, 2004, 2003 & 2001
- Regional Pairs Champion (10) 2020, 2018, 2015, 2011, 2008, 2006, 2005, 2004, 2002 & 2001
- Regional Mixed Pairs Champions (1) 2020
- Regional Triples Champion (7) 2016, 2015, 2008, 2007, 2006, 2005 & 2004
- Regional Fours Champion (4) 2018, 2015, 2011 & 2010

Club Championships (61)
- Singles (13) 2019, 2018, 2017, 2016, 2013, 2012, 2011, 2009, 2008, 2007, 2006, 2004 & 2002
- Pairs (13) 2020, 2019, 2018, 2017, 2016, 2015, 2014 (twice), 2012, 2010, 2009, 2008 & 2005
- Mixed Pairs (2) 1996, 2007
- Triples (11) 2019, 2017, 2016, 2015, 2011, 2010, 2006, 2005, 2004, 2002 & 2001

- Fours (12) 2019, 2018, 2017, 2016, 2015, 2014, 2012, 2010, 2009, 2008, 2004 & 2003
- Major/Minor Pairs (1) 2016
- 21 Up, 100 Up, 2 bowl singles (9) from 1999-2007

Total: 137 titles at club, regional, State, and National level

Pennant Premierships (8)
- Bendigo East (BBD Division 1) 2018/19
- Essendon (Melbourne Premier Division) 2015/16
- Glenorchy-Rodman (Hobart Premier) 2014/15
- Brighton (Melbourne Division 1) 2010/11
- Karingal (Nepean Premier Division) 2007/2008
- Bundoora (Melbourne Premier Division) 2004/05
- Bundoora (Melbourne Division 1) 2001/02
- Altona (Melbourne Premier Division) 2000/01